But maybe it's time to let all this go. The naming and the wrestling. (Judgment.) The naming and the renaming of the self.

Maybe it's time instead for the giving over of the self.

Ahsahta Press
Boise, Idaho

The New Series #75
2017

OBJECTS FROM A BORROWED CONFESSION

JULIE CARR

Ahsahta Press, Boise State University, Boise, Idaho 83725-1525
Cover design by Quemadura / book design by Janet Holmes
ahsahtapress.org

LIBRARY OF CONGRESS CATALOGING-IN-PUBLICATION DATA

Names: Carr, Julie, 1966– author.
Title: Objects from a borrowed confession / Julie Carr.
Description: Boise, Idaho : Ahsahta Press, 2016. | Series: The new series ; #75 |
Includes bibliographical references.
Identifiers: LCCN 2016040886 (print) | LCCN 2016049541 (ebook) | ISBN 9781934103708 (Paperback) |
ISBN 1934103705 (Paperback)
Subjects: LCSH: Self-disclosure. | Emotions. | Identity (Psychology) | Intimacy (Psychology) | Self.
Classification: LCC PS3603.A77425 .A6 2016 (print) | LCC PS3603.A77425 (ebook) | DDC 818/.609—dc23
LC record available at https://lccn.loc.gov/2016040886

THIS BOOK IS DEDICATED TO

K.J. HOLMES

Contents

*What do we want to know
and how far are we willing to go to get it?
A novella*

Dear J.

I've been meaning to write to you for some time, though I am sure you are surprised to hear from me. I think we're not much alike. At the time of our closest connection, you were tall, narrow, and quiet in a long coat—very elegant. I was distraught but doubt I looked it, practicing handstands on subway platforms. I hung out with the one angled between us and you did not, but actually, one could say it was the other way around—he went home with me and thought of you. For this reason I couldn't speak to you when we ran into each other at events, I wouldn't look at you unless it was always, and then I did, across rooms shut tight against traffic moving models and billboards, freezing them in air. I thought you beautiful in ways I could not be. I also thought that you were cruel. But it wasn't cruelty you carried but an irresistible sense of tragedy (it has to be mentioned). There was something about a bridge: the two of you walking across it in the wind. I think it was there, on that bridge, that you revealed your motherless status—

Dear J.

Today our x's name is splayed across the nation. On screens and papers, in mouths everywhere. How do you feel about this? I can only imagine as an early snow falls. His scandal is the occasion, but not the reason, for my writing to you. I wanted to know something about you—were you a mother, were you alone. I've wanted to know that you are happy. At one time I wanted the force of our accumulative happiness, yours and mine, to reduce his to a ball of lead sitting at the bottom of a granite quarry unexamined for eternity. Now I just imagine you and I joining hands on an airplane headed to visit the fusion reactor in Aix, or dancing close at some party in a granary. I imagine these things and then I recoil from them.

"The sky and earth in their lust seem small on this naked body of water" writes the ancient Vietnamese poet. His subject here, as always, is envy.

Dear J.

I write in the morning: a fly and a glare. And I "try to show you what is inside myself—a freak, a foible, a mental illness if you like."

In light like this, I should try better to reveal my motives, but that I'm not sure I know them to show them. Is it that you should have been my daughter rather than my rival? If we were hit by the same strong wind, I should have been the one to protect you? No tears. "I admit I hide out in the office," the x confessed once the two of you were finally off in the City of Magnificent Distances. How and why did this communication occur? I report this not in order to hurt you, but to reveal to you what hides. I am trying only to uncover what's been concealed for so long, and if I happen to express contempt, even disgust for the past, you will forgive me? But J., everything you read is a reflection—and so you will need to forgive not me, but yourself.

Today my ten-year-old daughter told me, while doing some Lady Gaga moves in the kitchen, that she had just two things to look forward to: owning a credit card and sitting in the front seat. She has other things to look forward to, worthy things, as you and I know, or as I hope you know, because I cannot tell, looking at your photos, what you know, which is why, maybe, I am writing. "Nothing," writes Flaubert in the mind of Emma Bovary, "was worth the trouble of seeking it; everything was a lie. Every smile hid a yawn of boredom, every joy a curse, all pleasure satiety, and the sweetest kisses left upon your lips only the unattainable desire for a greater delight." Maybe, J., I just want to prove to you that she is wrong.

There is no harm in speaking of the past, for the past does not exist, is less than the light that falls toward my face. The future, however, is a red fox, running right past me, headed for the dark hole where it lives. Or else it's like the flush in Emma Bovary's cheeks: fleeting, alluring, and unsure of its cause.

Dear J.

We looked at one another across a classroom. We were in a soft box. We're in one now. There's a lot that doesn't happen. We aren't in a field or a river. We aren't naked. We are not the children of communists. Nor are we loved by religious grandmothers. Our light is ugly. We are worried about words. We don't touch one another's wrists. J., I know nothing of the party happening in your head, I can see only your body, and that only in my mind. I don't cause myself physical pain. This is better theater, more believable, stronger. There's water in the bottle and charge in the machine. I have no requirement to speak of anything in particular. I ask you to look back at me, and that's all. Someone else might make a play about his father. Someone else might sing, "born to be wild." I do this; and if I happen to express adoration for an absence, you will forgive me? You will forgive yourself.

J.

"I've written about this quite often over the years, but I always forget it. I am my brain. Whenever I remember this . . . the thought simultaneously fills me with horror and wonder, while also raising all sorts of ethical questions as to how I should live my life."

That is not something I wrote, it's something I read on a blog. Here we have the ultimate question that all materialists face: once the human is understood as only matter, where do we find our imperatives? Thinking of ourselves as a cluster of synapses, as a function of electrical currents running through "one form among many" stripped of soul, we are left as only "Mill or Machine," to quote William Blake.

But I am not a materialist, as my reaching back through time to touch you must prove. For example, my son has just turned fourteen and all of my advice to him is derived from the philosophy of Andy Warhol: "Fantasy love is much better than reality love"; "Never doing is very exciting." I wouldn't say these are rules to live by, but they help.

This morning a Parisian man, retired manager of an animation studio, sits in my basement sipping tea. Today I will sweat through a few museums with him for company. I know that you are a historian now, which I really respect. For me, it's important to respect you, to choose you, in a sense, as an object in my mind. Somewhere someone wrote that there is nothing more horrifying than the thoughts that slip away. We want to be "part of the earth" and yet, this "perpetual vanishing" of ourselves. We have an experience and we think we "survive" it, but what is this self that survives? A set of habits? A voice? A voice that others recognize? Dear J., I do not know your voice. I could say that a goal of mine is to know your voice.

"What kind of being am I," asks the blogger-philosopher, "that I am *making* myself in the activity of thinking and remembering?"

And I, in thinking, in remembering, am I making you?

J.

I am my brain. But is this true, a simple truth, when yesterday I found almost each man in the café to be an object of some vague desire? And all because the barista, a skinny small-nosed boy in a band, smiled at me? His little smile, though only the smile of one who wanted a tip, gave me access to the world of girls who might be his fans, who might actually end up sleeping with him. This access occurred in my bloodstream, which is to say I did not exactly experience it as a thought, or even as a nervous tinge, though of course it had thinking elements, which is why I can tell you about it. This sharp if unfocused transitory sensation did not seem a very important part of me, of my day, but it was a bit more important later when a more appropriately aged fantasy lover asked me to watch his iPad while he peed.

Where am I going with this? It says something about fashion. About the power of the male body. It says more about the images the mind makes as it translates the blood's pulse. Some filmmakers I met at a party last night had horrible hair. Big and ragged, tightly glued to their scalps, or growing in greasy clumps that hung across their faces. As if making pleasing images by day, they had to refuse them at night. Or as if they believed the premise too much: I am my brain. Or as if, J., they were as frightened by beauty as I am of you.

J.

Today I read about the inventor of chemical warfare. I read about chlorine gas, mustard gas and the gas that damages, not your body, but your brain. When you are exposed to this gas you are stripped of your will to participate in even the most mundane tasks. You hear the groans of others, but you cannot hear yourself groaning. You see that they are in pain, but you cannot feel your own pain. The colors of the world become all one color. Thought dissolves into a fluid-form belonging to anyone.

J., it's been a bad day full of semi-enclosed spaces and too much parental guidance. You do not have to like me, but think of me as an eager affection fixed against reason, as something that resists.

The secrets under the hat are a kind of fuel for me, driving this incessant interest in letters. Every day resolves itself in language, like insects running across snow, or like the premonitions of Philip Glass heard through a pillow.

Words are talismans. I've never been so happy/frightened/ sad.

Dear J.

I've been distracted—pulled from my attention to our bond by the intrusions of various chlorides, various crises of national and international scale, to say nothing of domestic. The facts are such that at times I bow to them like a princess to an abusive king. I'm hoping, as I tell of these facts, that you will hear me as a priest hears his confessor—in the dark.

Another child has been shot and killed. Mother of him spoke to the nation, to the unborn too, saying, give them back. Elsewhere four men approached a woman on a bus. Through her asshole they've damaged, fatally, her intestines. As they raped her, J., they beat her with blunt objects. But what could these be? Phones? Bricks? I don't know.

A piece of meat is the body? In order to understand this, we conduct our searches, but our search options appear limited. We type the words "boy shot" and are given the following choices:

> boy shot in head
> boy shot with crossbow
> boy shot with pellet gun
> boy shot six times
> boy shot by cop
> boy shot in school
> boy shot by cop in school

You see what I am, what we are, together?

J.

Today's star ledger: Neptune and Venus begin to slide from one another slowly as if the spreading fingertips of your widening hand. Clench your fist at arms length and you'll fill the space between them. Venus, the arbiter of love, beauty, and sex drifts toward Mars—military power, violence, and fear—they'd never really been apart. Skirts thunder.

Dear J.

As often happens, I woke up thinking of you.

Last night I arrived home from an art opening to a house of mournful looking children and scraps of food left in bowls lying around in various rooms. Piercing looks revealed nothing, but as I was drinking my coffee this morning, preparing to write to you, I discovered I'd left a tab open on my computer. I'd been searching "bladder cancer" and hadn't closed the tab, thinking there were a few points I needed to bring up with my urologist, an upbeat thirtyish person called Amanda. J., it's basically a given that I don't have bladder cancer, but I am going through a rite of passage.

One has to wonder, maybe you are wondering, at the unexplored or undisclosed reasons one might leave such a tab open? It's not as if I'm trying to garner morbid attention from my own children, is it? The one thing I can say about the work at the art opening is that it lacked urgency. These days, the dominant aesthetic in my city is amusement—pleasant unpressured and only slightly ironic. The very pregnant composer leaned against a railing and declared herself disdainful of "normal people." But that was as edgy as it got.

But the too-pleasant art opening coupled with the sulkily scared children bring me again to what I think of today as my calling: *to hold your image in my mind and try to see into it*. It's as if you're a dead person I'm trying to recall, as in, call back to life.

You had a look of struck horror, or struck sorrow (it went back and forth) on your face. I think you'd been wearing that look since infancy. What does an infant know about its mother's death? Everything, evidently. A friend of mine whose father died when she was two has no such look. Mostly she looks like a mom (a look I happen to like), but sometimes, like when introducing herself to the curator in the elevator, she looks like a capable, game and brainy kid. Not mournful, not shocked. But you, in those years, seemed never to shed that look. Though the wiki on bladder cancer scares me less than it might, it did temporarily paste that look onto my daughters' eyes.

That look—which was your look—which I so prefer to the cheerful faces of people approaching amusing art—I'm holding it in my mind, trying to see into it in order to know something about a mother's death, about—maybe—my own.

J.

I hold you in my mind and I try to see into you. It's like trying to see into all of womankind. That's ridiculous, though Melville would OK it. My mother would have too, though she was one of those feminists who scorned words like "womankind." Not because she preferred "mankind," but because, like the pregnant composer in the museum, she didn't want to be associated with women particularly. Not with "normal" women anyway. I seem to be floating off my point again like a rowboat unable to dock. It's like this: I am a woman. This is a thought that passes my mind a thousand times a day and occupies my mind as I sleep. This might be, actually, the most persistent thought I have. With my legs crossed to protect my sex, shielding the specificity of being female, I taste that. Perhaps a man feels this way too—constantly hearing the phrase "I am a man." But I doubt it. If he says so, J., he's probably lying.

But we've all fucked a liar. And maybe we had to in order to prepare ourselves for our tasks, for a liar is a catalyst, less a person than a woman is. A liar, though seeming to hide his depth in secrets, actually has no depth. I will return to this.

Dear J.

I escape the pains of the present by re-examining the pains of the past. As I rode the bus home from another x's apartment—I was almost a child—I didn't yet drive—my body sometimes involuntarily jumped, as if either sex or shame created spasms in my nerves. This was not pleasant, but it wasn't unpleasant either. Like lying, it created in me the feeling, false I now know, that I was following my own fate, a fate I couldn't control but which would one day reveal its logic to me.

Did you have that sense too when you turned as panoramic as an air raid and I couldn't get out from under?

And were you to blame?

There are, in life, competing passions. And perhaps we choose which ones to live in, or perhaps we only narrate the past.

Later I would try to imagine my own bad behaviors as motivated by something other than the desire for revenge, a sort of freedom. But there was no other deeper motive than this desire for freedom won through cruelty. What had been done to me, what had been done to my mother, this I would now do to others. As if all men were one man and all women me.

J., all the ways in which I've hurt others have made those others more beautiful to me.

I know exactly how that sounds. But this has been true for a dozen years, and was true before then, though I didn't know it, and might also be true for you.

J:

For a while I found it only an amusement, imagining your pristine home and history books, or picturing you with an infant on some Italian island like H.D. Then something changed and that scarf you always wore took root in my mind. I was afraid that crying on the subway or puncturing your body with needles, you had become the performance artist I always wanted to be, had settled down in Germany or somewhere else where ugliness is a virtue. I imagined taking up smoking and walking along the Muddy River with you at dusk. I thought about sitting on the hood of a car with you like it was the seventies again, a cat in the car's shade. This isn't an erotic narrative, but it is a passion. In the basement of a piano showroom you beat your drums. I don't say much. I tie my shoe.

I have discovered this need to break something, even if it's only something fragile, like a fly's wing. Narrowing my eyes, tightening my jaw—this is my way of reaching you and it could go on for decades. I've kept my pulse pretty steady through all of it, except when I think of you calling me by my full name. It's like this:

1. If I claim never to have admired you, I will lose the part of myself that misses you
2. and so will miss that part of myself

Dear J.

You write that though many of my insights are sharp and true, in folding the past into the present, I am confusing pleasure with pain, peace with war. (Though you didn't really write that, I can deduce it from things you have written, not to me in particular, to your friends.) But J., though you might fairly respond with suspicion and distrust, I'm going for nothing less than what James Agee called "the cruel radiance of what is."

Spitting, jittery, oddly sexy, was the "Cambridge Marxist" who said, shaking his leg, wiping his lip of sweat, "It has to hurt you," with a Britishy emphasis on the "hurt"—his r so far forward in his mouth as to be nearly inaudible to an American ear. It has to "huuut" you. The "it" in his sentence is writing.

I woke up this morning with you and that phrase together in my mind.

Today, J., an allegory:

There was once a miller who had a beautiful daughter, and as she was grown up, he wished her to be wed. So poor was this miller that any suitor would do. "Any suitor" he said to himself, "that asks for her, I will give her to him." Not long after, a suitor came who appeared to be very rich. The miller could find no fault with him and gave his daughter over. The girl, however, did not like this man quite so much as a girl should like the man to whom she is engaged. Whenever she saw or thought of him, she felt a secret horror.

One day the man said to the girl, "You are my betrothed, and yet you have never once paid me a visit." The girl replied, "I know, I've been so busy!" But the bridegroom insisted, "My house is out there in the dark forest." She said she could not find her way. The bridegroom said, "But you must come. I've already invited the guests. I will strew ashes in order that you may find it." Sunday came, the day of the gathering, and the girl set out, following the trail of dust.

She walked almost the whole day until she reached the middle of the forest where she found a solitary house, dark and dismal. She went inside, but no one was within, and the most absolute stillness reigned. Suddenly, a voice cried out: "Turn back, turn back! 'Tis a murderer's house you enter here!" The voice was a bird's, a bird trapped inside a cage. Again it cried, "Turn back, turn back, 'Tis a murderer's house!"

The girl walked from one room to another, but not one human being could she find. At last she came to the cellar, and there sat an extremely aged woman whose head shook constantly.

"Poor child," said the old woman, "you are in a murderer's den. Look, I have been forced to put a great kettle on. When they have you in their power, they will cut you to pieces without mercy, will cook you and eat you, for they are eaters of human flesh. If I do not have compassion for you and save you, you will be lost."

J., it's for these two, this young woman wandering, this old woman quivering, that I write this now.

J.

A city in the rain, I am alone. My letters to you lead nowhere. Nowhere universal and nowhere even broad.

I've been distracted again, first by one disease and then by another. A friend of mine and a friend of your friend, or our friend, may not be dying but will be receiving "all they have in terms of treatment."

I want not the slightest coppery tinge of irony in my voice here. What does it mean to say, "I love you" to this woman, our mutual friend and our friend's friend, with this disease? I love all the women who write, I think. I am picturing your body and hers. If, as the socialist on the radio said, human beings are as likely to care for one another as they are to harm one another, is my picturing of your body and her body a form of care or of harm? To rest my face on her or your belly, to kiss the white or brown skin, to touch your or her face, would be an act that serves whom, exactly?

A freckle between her shoulder blades. I keep trying to zip it into my mind.

Two days ago, before I heard the news of our friend, I floated down the Platte River with my four-year-old resting on my chest. With one hand I stroked her hair; with the other I paddled. Sharp blue sky and pink rock formations drifted by. I said, "This is Heaven on Earth," though it was not. It was and it was not.

We were hiding, though she didn't know this, from the fires and the seas, from the wars and the shooters. Is all of earth "Heaven on Earth" she wanted to know? No, it is not, I said. And so we listed the places that are not: the boring places and the sad ones. The places where people have "no fun."

Dear J.

Late summer now, marked by the travels of others, the splendor of always-arriving photographs from "Japan," "Paris: Montmartre," "Carcassonne!" or "Lima"—they all look like disaster shots to me. For I approach the world now from the point of view of "summers without flowers, daughters without mothers, and sea without produce."

This first sharp morning gilds a fallen plumb. I found a crayon in the basement the color of your hair. As repellent as a flashbulb are the fingernails of the dead.

J., the cool wooden table I rest my wrists on—it goes on beyond me. To this only I will dedicate myself. And to you.

"Silence is everywhere," as Flaubert writes.

Dear J.

Is retyping the words of someone you have lost or are afraid of losing, or of someone you wanted but never had, a way to resist this loss, this never-having?

Maybe you've retyped the words of your mother? Words found in diaries or letters? Mine wrote me a card shortly before she could no longer write. "I am proud of you," she wrote, "but mostly I want you to know what a good daughter you have always been." These are not her precise words. Her precise words are tucked into a red box inside a closet I cannot open. Next week she'll be moved from one home to another home. My stepfather visits her daily to prepare her for this move. Though there is no language, there might be eye contact, briefly, and there is always touch.

That bit of blue in the sky seems, at dawn, unable to fully assert itself. But who knows?

Dear J.

October now and the busses suck the children up in the morning, spit them back out again at four. It has been a while, then, since my last note. And though I've missed you, I'm losing the urge to write to you. No longer is my question: what is a woman, as the trees heave in wind. And no longer is my question: how can I love you? I have other questions now and I doubt you can help me with them.

I've wanted to know you—not exactly "know" (smell, or taste?)—in order to understand everything I did not understand about the feminine. This must be a common desire: if one's lover chooses another, one is inclined also to long for that other body in order to understand whatever it is one seems to lack. But I suspect, and I don't say this to be hurtful, that it was not your body that drew him—it was your grief, even as twenty-year-old grief can harden into a kind of chill. There's more to you than this body and this grief, I know that. There's also your intellect. But I'm surrounded by intellects. What I don't have is a woman's body to taste or smell. One cannot taste or smell an image, even a moving one. Yesterday, a rusted piece of edging I yanked from the ground, Russian sage, chlorine on my skin, and a whole array of scents at the salon: none of these seemed to emanate from a body. Later: salt, coffee, a fig. Even then I lacked another flavor.

But what I wanted to say to you today was that I no longer imagine these information centers to reside in you. My original impulses—to apologize for hating you, to find a way to like you—have been satisfied. This newer impulse, the most driving impulse of all, to know "your" or "a" or "any" body—cannot be fulfilled.

"The love I suffer is a shameful disease," says Apollinaire.

Dear J.

I'm writing again, after months of nothing, on this the first day of a new year, with a confession: I allowed my daughter and her friends to watch *Psycho* at her slumber party. I had no guilt, I *wanted* them, for reasons I didn't at the time think about, to see that mother in the basement: her empty skull propped on her clothed and rotting corpse.

This mistake, if it was a mistake, has cost my daughter at least one friend—that is, if the friend's mother has anything to do with it. I wanted to shout, not at that mother, but at the world, maybe at you: better that they see the rotting corpse of the mother than the dozens of fleshy girls parading themselves before panels of judging "sales associates" and "friends" in *Say Yes to the Dress*— where they submit, as I had, to the regime of "self-improvement" with the goal of acquiring the male, the children, who will then all be submitted to similar rituals of dressing, redressing, presenting and representing themselves before ever-widening circles of judges for ever more violent reconstructions.

That, J., is the true horror show. The dead mother is only all of ours, the dead mother we carry from room to room—we dress her and speak to her, we shout at and whisper to her—she must be dragged from the basement into the light of day, not so we can finally bury her, but so we can finally admit our love for her, how we care for her, how we speak in her voice, how finally, we become her.

J.

It was a summer when I first wrote to you, and now it is a summer again. That summer—dry grasses out my window, little birds pecking—I thought quite a lot about you. Now I never think of you.

But last night, driving a friend home along the highway, listening to her speak bitterly about her x ("What's wrong with him?" and, "I've spent too much time thinking about what's wrong with him.") while fireworks flooded various skies, I thought again about you and our shared bond. I thought too about the risks one takes when writing about "other people." I put that in quotations marks, as I'm sure you understand, because, like dreams, writing is only about you.

Drawing on memory or invention, I place us back in a minor gallery. bell hooks is talking about race and feminism, and I think you understand better than I do what's being said. There might be references to Marx or to other feminists I have not read. Mostly, in rooms like that, I felt worried. Mouth at an angle, darkness at the window. Coats on chairs, on laps, on the floor.

Those were years of activism. I was on my bike, you were in your long coat with velvet trim, and you were and were not my "sister." When two women stare at one another through the body of another, the gaze can be a symptom of pain or of its opposite.

Forcing ourselves into rooms crowded with angry men, some of whom were dying, many of whom are now dead—sitting around conference tables with shy scholars gazing down—or seated in auditoriums for award ceremonies aimed at others—we took notes, always, in our bright little notebooks. At that time a hard cock was more annoyance than pleasure. Food was similarly problematic. If I said we were doing the work of "growing up" would that sound right to you? Or did you consider yourself already grown?

J., because you stood for tragedy, a motherless girl, a sad one, I was afraid.

The room fogs up. A slice of lemon pie, untouched and glistening sweats alone on its plate. It's for you, just for you.

Objects from a Borrowed Confession

Now to bring my body back into the present

I try to see into the faces of the dead.

They are people who want to be in your life, deep in your life, even when they say they don't.

Don't touch my back.

It wasn't "true," it wasn't real life, but then in the morning, it was.

During the most intensive week of editing the journal titled, "The Shape of the I," Destin Self, a five-year-old boy, dies in an accident at home.

The writers speak of the self as a blend between narcissus and echo, as in need of passionate attachments, as unable to give up the notion that it was born for a reason, as not a person but one side of the compound word "healthcare." Someone is always talking: "I'm a phony fuck just like my Dad"; "The text signs itself on my behalf"; "O, ambivalent plural being."

Destin Self liked the Children's Museum and he liked to play "puppies" with Lucy. How might it be possible to "compose" a common world? The downturn aggravates this trend toward tragedy.

"No one has the slightest idea what will work," says the politician in the face of more losses. "The cupboard is bare."

At the memorial for five-year-old Destin Self a man with a black beard, leather jacket and bald head weeps silently into his hands. Destin's mother wears her hair in eight evenly spaced knots, her pink scalp a grid of skin.

His grandmother kisses her own hands and holds them up to the ceiling of the Children's Museum's Activity Room.

That night I dream the son of a great poet is staying at our house while we travel north for a while. Regardless of his parentage, he has to pay the rent.

His girlfriend, an artist, asks if I think anyone is buying art these days and I say, on my way to the garden with a trowel, I doubt it.

They'll have to borrow to pay but I don't care. My father, the guy tells me, probably wrote some poems in this house back in the year such-and-such when he visited here. That's nice, I answer, not impressed.

They've taken the bloody sheet off the bed. It's my blood, so it doesn't really disgust me, but they didn't wash it, just stashed it in the area where their junk is.

His father, the great poet, he was a drunk. There'll be blood in the house again, I think, but it won't be my blood this time, and I'm worried about that. That's why I need the $1,400.

It's California so it's sunny all the time no matter what's going on with blood and poverty. Ruth tells me on the phone, people who stay in your house do weird things like glue your pots together (we laugh).

I plant oleander along the fence.

Tim's already up north. I'd be with him by now, but had to go back for some papers. That's how I found them cooking in the kitchen, that's why I saw the blood, and then, more blood.

"Is the boy dead, or is this a dream?" I ask them, letting my arms hang.

"I think," they say very gently, "it's a memory."

This story is about a girl named Goldilocks-Jacklyn.

Goldilocks-Jacklyn met a monster. The monster had glue on his mouth. In order to get the glue off he uses tape. But then the tape sticks too, so now he has both glue and tape on his mouth. Goldilocks-Jacklyn says to the monster, "Can you talk?" The monster says, "Mmmm." "Is that all you can say?" asks Goldilocks-Jacklyn. "Duh," says the monster.

And this one is for Mama Jeet:

Some turn this way and some turn that way.

Some are whipped for stealing a pig and are not inclined toward reconciliation.

"I should be desirous to whisper into the ear of our governor, to identify all thugs and ter-rorists, but induced to the utmost misery and wretchedness, I see no end and no reason," writes one such one in his / destroyed diary.

After seven months of habitation in a permafrost, they nevertheless summon

the dull and grainy politics of passivity.

The tape recorder picks up the voices of the dead, reproduces what we refuse to represent.

The camera spills their faces onto the ground or, howling, back into our air.

In the morning after the gunshots:

how badly I want to move on, but to what? To the island of Noxos?

At the memorial we learn that Destin liked to blow bubbles in the snow.

This is a document of poverty and bad luck I wrote with my

fingers.

A painted stone holds the employment eligibility verification form from Homeland Secu-

rity to the desk. I've practiced only

an ineffective strategy of resistance

as is known by the mother

of Destin Self.

"Jaffe's mom gives her chocolate in her lunch each day, cleans her room for her and makes her bed,"

she says, dipping her belongings into salt

and then licking each one.

She wants to visit Destin's stone. She makes me look him up on the Internet to see if we can locate it.

She makes me look once in the morning and then again at the end of the day. Nope, I tell her, there's no information about Destin online. But, she says, maybe the computer is still looking?

Again from her bed: When can we go see Destin's stone? She wants to know if she can bring the stone home. No, I say. It has to stay there. It's big and it's in the ground. Does it have his name on it? Yes. When I die will you visit my stone? You won't die, I say. Or, I'll die first. You'll die? Yes, I say, with firm satisfaction. We will die first.

But who will be my parents?
You won't need parents. I am a little bit
malicious.

Next a dream of a very short man dancing on stage.

A drunk veteran heckling from the back.

Two women, one a beauty leaning toward bitter, the other more "librarian," stand

to watch. It's not just that he's small, he also has no legs, and his arms, on which

he supports himself, are really only stumps. And then from behind us comes the

taunt: "How do you know where to tickle him?" More a child's question than an

insult, but we know the drunk's intentions. "Quiet!" I yell, to no use. He's going

on with other taunts, loud and out of control, until another blonde stands and

throws him in the drier. That does it; but that a drier, I happen to know, can kill

a person. We listen to him screaming and thumping around in there, and then I

get worried and charge over, but not before I tell blonde-get-it-done to call 911,

which she refuses to do.

I drag this drunk and now unconscious marine from the drier, afraid to check

his pulse. He begins to come-to, to twitch awake. Grateful and relieved, I look up.

And in the paper, the 2,000th American soldier has died in Afghanistan. A boy named

Lance (and how many unnamed?). His parents, crying and gripping the flag on the front

page, are no older than me.

Was this an image of the divine or of hell?

An historian in a café thinks about the destruction of boundaries in mining accidents, the uncertainty surrounding the border between the living and dead, how the bosses had to get dead bodies out of the ground in order to place them again into the ground, this historian in his beige pants and yellowish jacket says he doesn't go by the concept of truth but instead, verisimilitude—which he defines as the spinning of tales we can believe in. What has he got to build his tales on? The bloodied ground, the rotting corpses of donkeys.

The historian is seated at a tall table, wearing blue.

"We should aim at the Infinite but tangentially, rebounding on the curvature of light in order to change planets," he writes optimistically.

Eyes of a girl watch me from across the room. Like a lifeguard, someone young is always following me, insisting on bodies in space.

How far from some images I want to camp. But if language matters more, then how does this language move? It moves away. So what kind of worship is this?

But are the heavens, as we see them, or imagine them, a sphere that surrounds us (in which case there are other spheres surrounding other planets) or a single sphere surrounding everything, which will never end its outward expansion?

"We might say the sky is on the side of the open," says a philosopher who's being recorded speaking to children. "Whereas on the earth," he explains, "everything is always closed." I don't know about that. Is everything on earth always closed? Your hands, for example, or the curve of your skull, closed? He doesn't back off his claim. This might be because he's speaking to children and doesn't want to complicate things, though children seem the least likely to make this distinction between "open" and "closed." How could things be thought of as "stopping" at their edges?

She asks whether she might go back inside my body for a while. When I say no, she considers my refusal to be nothing but a misunderstanding. She will, she explains, reenter my body later when she is very old. My body she considers "open," time also "open."

God, the philosopher tells the children, is not in the world, which is to say, not part of the universe that we could travel through with our spacecraft, see with our telescopes. God is somewhere that is nowhere, something that is nothing. This, as my friend puts it, is a summary of "the laborious opera concerning how we came to name the eternal."

Therefore the question "Does God exist" is the wrong question.

The answer for religious and non-religious people is the same: no. God does not "exist," is an object constructed not according to truth but verisimilitude. A literary truth. What exists, says the philosopher to the children, are relationships between us humans, and also the idea of nothingness. These relationships can be more or less activated; we can think about them a lot, or only a little. Also, all of us can think about nothing when we want to. Everyone can entertain the idea of "nothingness" as easily as they can think about their mother. As easily as they can think about their son. A process is always distinct from its products. But whether thinking about it, imagining it, or refusing to, we're always in some relationship with this nothing, and so, though God does not exist, it also does not not exist, and so God is, if we want to say "is," always on the side of the sky, with the open open.

All that stands between myself and apples is nothing, he says.

Then the voices of humans begin to echo through that space, to fill it.

The War Reporter: On Confession

I started to write memoirs, addressing them to you, since I am always talking to you . . . if there are

any rests left, on paper, of my life, they will have to be like this, disjointed and uncertain, done for no

reason, and put in an envelope to mail.

—Martha Gellhorn, 1941 (*Letters* 117)

I.

What is it that I'm turning toward in turning toward you?

This is a question for philosophers: "What is it that I love in loving you?" asks St. Augustine of his

silent confessor (*Confessions* X: 6:8).

Or, more recently:

> May I say that you test me, that you yoke me to the trail of writing this confession in your
>
> silence so as to be assured that, wavering on the thread run out between yourself and
>
> myself, I do not fall back into the arrogance of being me without you, in my nothingness?
>
> (Lyotard, *Confessions* 75–76)

Confessing, does one ask to be forgiven? Or instead, to be recognized, even, one could say, *made*, made something rather than remaining (alone and) nothing?—Confessing do we admit to a failure or a desire?

*

Here are two confessional forms: the diary entry and the letter. T. J. Clark's *The Sight of Death*, recommended to me by my friend Stephen Goldsmith as he was mourning his father, later found ghosting the pages of Susan Howe's elegiac *That This*, and comprised of diary entries written in the sight of two paintings by seventeenth-century French painter Nicolas Poussin over a period of six months, opens by appealing to the reader for patience, sympathy:

> Perhaps I should register at least an awareness that this study of two pictures by Poussin seems to sit somewhat oddly with the other main piece of writing I have been involved with over the past two years . . .Some readers, I suspect, will not understand, and maybe not sympathize . . . . (vii-viii)

The initial undated diary entry, which functions as an introduction, holds a bolder confession, this time of depression or simply bad mood:

> I was in low spirits—irritated at my own irritation . . . I kept thinking of William Morris's great tirade against Queen Victoria's Golden Jubilee, and felt ashamed of my own incapacity for anger. I badly needed something better to think about. (1)

In this way the book claims intimacy with its reader, its "you." In this way it acknowledges that what its writer most needs is some new access to liveliness, some way to reawaken—through the acts of looking and writing—a kind of presence.

Martha Gellhorn's letters, by nature of their form, are in almost all moments intimate, often reaching toward their various readers with intense loneliness. They confess to many things: to self-loathing, impatience, love, to doubts of all kinds. But mostly they confess to the desire to be alive—for liveliness in spite of, in the face of, in sight of, death.

*

> I do think you would wish very much to have seen, the other afternoon, the tiny little silver balloons like elephants floating against a pink red sky over the city that is now so shabby and still quite lovely. I think you would have liked the black Lancs going off into the black night. I think you would like the cold long train rides, listening to the people talk. I think it is not disgusting to look at the world and at the war; because someone must see, and after all we have trained ourselves to see. (Gellhorn 159)

Gellhorn is trying to convince Ernest Hemingway to join her in London two years after the Blitz and six months before D-Day. "I think it is not disgusting to look at the world and at the war," she says, presumably because he's indicated some disgust (after all, she is a woman and his wife), or maybe because, though the war is disgusting, the act of looking is a way to live, a way to, if not defy, then at least *accompany* the disgust that is war. We know that she would soon leave "E," as she called him, later referring to their marriage as a kind of torture. This letter is one of many that exhibit the desperate longing we sometimes feel for people we're about to abandon. But what's important is not her confessed desire for him (which seems forced anyway), but her desire to include him, or anyone, in the things she sees: the balloon, the pink sky, the black night, the black Lancs.

In letter after letter she details her ongoing effort and need to, through the act of seeing and saying what she sees, become a part of what is—"I would give anything on earth to be part of the invasion and see Paris right at the beginning . . ." (159)—as if only attention, first-hand witnessing, counts as living. "I see perfection as a complete aliveness; being alert and eager" (21), she writes. Her confessional impulse is intense and ongoing, not unlike our own.

*

But is there, in seeing and describing what one sees, in attempting to "tell the truth"—to say what is—an ethics? This is what Clark argues (and the young Gellhorn too, though later, she gives up on it). Serving as eyes for others is more than a professional duty. It is, to borrow Clark's other term for it, "a politics."

"We are in a war," writes Clark, a war of "representations and actions . . . and part of the struggle at present is simply to save the possibility of truth—of complexity and humanity—in either sphere, and in the spheres' constant overlapping" (115).

This "possibility of truth" —it's what close looking or close reading and the careful descriptions they give rise to hope to approach. It's what confession hopes to achieve. Against this, we have the constant "regime of visual flow," what Clark calls a "pseudo-utopia present[ing] itself as the very form of self-knowledge . . ." (15). Such lies, argues Clark, are devastating because, like a changeling staring up from the cradle, they've replaced the human.

Battling, then, on the side of truth and humanity—his only weapons, eyes with which to see, language with which to describe—the art writer turns soldier.

The young Gellhorn also saw "the act of keeping the record straight" as a necessary good, as, in a sense, salvational. Gellhorn too was fighting on the side of the human, telling the truth as a way of honoring, while war discards, both the living and the dead: "I lavish my heartaches all over the place: but I still know what I'm doing. I believe in man." "What happens to human beings, before during and after . . . [war], is all that matters" (61, 120).

And, as for Clark, her only weapon is description, telling what she sees, attention to the details of what is.

2.

But however compelled I am by this political humanist project, I return to another thought: That the ethics of seeing, of really seeing, and describing what one sees, this effort to tell some kind of truth (which is one way to define confessional writing) meets an opposing force—not just the lies that others tell, but the fact that the very thing most needing to be told remains outside of language.

To quote Amiri Baraka on the day after his death:

"I seen something / I SEEN something / And you seen it too / You just can't call its name" ("Something in the Way of Things")

To see into something that can't be seen, to name something that has no name, to speak to someone who cannot respond (in Lyotard's terms, "to bear witness" to "unpresentability")—this seems to me to be the other work of confession, the work that can never be finished, that keeps confession alive. Perhaps all the effort thrown into the act of seeing, of being alert to the present in whatever way one can ("a complete aliveness, being alert and eager"), might be less a way to "serve truth" than an attempt to experience present time as it is lost, an attempt to seize or stabilize temporal momentum and all it carries with it: memory, love, self.

"At thy bidding the moments fly by. Grant me in them, an interval." (Augustine II: 2:3)

For seeing and describing in both Gellhorn and Clark are at all times charged with loss, with proximity to death, with grief and its partner: desire. But this seems so often to be the case with confession: a death, or death in general, sits beside or within the urge to confess. As Derrida points out: "Augustine writes *Confessions* after his mother's death. Lyotard publishes posthumously his *The Confessions of St. Augustine*, I wrote 'Circumfession' while my mother was alive but not able to identify me, to recognize me, to name me, to call me" (Caputo 26). Barthes' *Mourning Diary*, written on the death of his mother: "Less and less to write, to say, except this (which I can tell no one)." Alice Notley's *In The Pines:* "Is that him dead, or is that me?"; "I was witness, I was his dead eyes" (3). Perhaps what must be confessed to, with death so nearby, listening in, is simply the fact of living, of life itself.

*

I wouldn't be writing this if I didn't also have something to confess. And what I confess to here is also nothing more or less than my aliveness. Why would I need to confess this: I am alive? Because I'm a child who outlives her mother.

*

And it's not just that I confess to being alive while she dies, guilty or ashamed in my body not for anything I've done, but simply for being, what I'll confess to "in the sight of death" is also always the longing to be "a part" not just of what is, but also of what isn't any longer—

confessing in sight of death to a desire for some way to cross the uncrossable barrier between "us" and "them"—all the dead that stare up without seeing from the mass grave that is the earth—or more precisely in my case "me" and "her." This is where confession becomes a kind of theology.

As Gerald Bruns says in his essay on Lyotard's *The Confessions of St. Augustine* (an impossible little book that itself stands on the border between the living and the dead, written on the eve of Lyotard's death):

> There is no separating theology from desire . . . . The God whom we experience is
> exactly the one who withholds himself from appearance and apprehension . . . leaving
> us to experience the absolute abjection of longing for what is untouchable, unnameable,
> unimaginable, unknowable, unthinkable, and deathly silent. (*Senses* 4)

*

Just before admitting that all the while as he's been gazing directly on his second and most important painting, "Landscape with a Man Killed by a Snake," he's been glancing sideways at a more intimate loss—the death of his mother—just before he admits that in fact it is her corpse that has

had his attention all along, Clark's confidence begins to falter:

> I feel resistance setting in at this point—my mind telling me I've gone far enough—but
>
> I shall blunder on, against all decency. I wonder if the ultimate horror surrounding the
>
> dead body . . . has to do with our sensing that all the identities and faces we are obliged
>
> to give the corpse . . . are no more than reaction-formations. They try to shield us from
>
> the great fact, the ultimate uncanny: that Death, in the corpse, disappoints us—looks
>
> away from us, and no longer has a face of any kind. (228)

"I've seen something / You've seen it too / You just can't call its name."

Confession, like all writing, "is always a matter of skirting around a black hole, the impenetrable,

the centrally mysterious" (Clark 164)[1].

----

[1] I think here of D.A. Miller's essay on Hitchcock's *Vertigo* in which Miller refers to the center of Madeleine's chignon as her "hairdo's black hole" (13). Later he will tie that black hole to the obscured, or perhaps absent, center of the film ("motiveless at its core" [13]), a film he claims to never be able to accurately remember or even follow. By his essay's end we understand that Miller's true subject here is memory itself, and the losses it holds. Vertigo is what we get when we attempt to locate something true and real in the present just as the past is pulling us back. In the end, Miller's essay is also a confession: confessing to nostalgia, to longing, and to how these states draw us vertiginously away from our own lives.

The "absolute abjection of longing" has no object, and that absence has only a false name, the name God for example, or the name mother, the name father. When I love you, what do I love? You try to name it; you can't name it.

"My patron said, 'name it'; // I said, I can not name it, there is no name." (H.D. *Trilogy* 76)

*

Last spring, before anything was really blooming, I found myself in Washington D.C. with a day alone. Largely because of Lyotard's essay "The Sublime and the Avant-Garde," but also just because of the paintings themselves, I went to see Barnett Newman's *Stations of the Cross*. Lyotard discusses these paintings as instances of the sublime "now," as an attempt to render in paint the rupture in time we could call "presence," a "now-ness" that "is a stranger to consciousness and cannot be constituted by it," a "now-ness" that can only be felt in the flesh, an aliveness (Lyotard "Sublime" 90).

The paintings were housed in a little room in the basement of the modern wing of the National Gallery. The room had a yellowish dank, under-lit feel, and was watched over by a guard afflicted with logomania—speaking incessantly into the wall before him, confessing, maybe, to nothing or everything. I tried, almost comically, to experience something at all, but my expectations had been too huge and the room too small. And so I went upstairs. I wandered around without purpose until finding myself in the rooms with the Impressionists. These paintings, achingly familiar from all kinds of commodities that have plastered them onto our eyes, were nothing to me. Until, it seemed, I suddenly looked up. And there was a color: a deep blue from my childhood: *Girl with Watering Can*, pinned to my wall for many years, until faded and curling at its edges. And then I knew I had been in this room before, forty years before as a three-year-old girl. My mother, having just separated from my father, had brought my brother and me for some weeks of recovery or reassessment (who knows?) to her parents' house in the city. Maybe she gave me the print that very day we saw the painting there, or maybe she bought it much later, remembering that I'd loved it. I thought the little girl on the path was myself. Or rather, I thought she was my daughter, my future daughter that I was bound to protect. And of course, standing there that day last spring, I started to cry, an odd kind of crying—a sudden burst that was as suddenly swallowed up by the quiet gallery and the silvery walls.

I went down to the gift shop and shamelessly purchased a card, sticking it into the book on Revolution that I'd been reading that week. A bookmark it remains.

*

One sees and in seeing, deeply attending, one feels one's "place in history" (again Gellhorn), or to put it more generally, one feels one's place in time—separate from any origin approaching some unknowable end, distinct from one's beloveds because one's beloveds are always distinct. Experiencing my place means I am here, which is to say, not there, not her, no longer her.

*

Confession as a mode of "harassing life in order to keep it alive" (Caputo 10).

*

There is in Lyotard's response to Newman a kind of rapture—"a painting by Newman is an angel" (79). The painting performs an annunciation, but what it announces is only presence itself. The verb "to be" becomes its own Utopic utterance. I have little to say about my little Renoir, but more to say about the way presence breaks in on you. You can't go looking for it, even less go shopping for it. In fact, you're in the way of it. "The course of real life, biography, gives lasting resistance to the improbable event of your coming," writes Lyotard or Augustine (it's impossible to tell) to their God (Lyotard *Confessions* 13). But then you find yourself standing, emerging out of shadows, arms by your sides, with whatever object you are holding, in her sight.

As Bruns writes, though consciousness cannot fully grasp the break in time we might call "nowness," the body knows only that pause: "The flesh belongs to the temporality of the meanwhile in which time does not pass but pauses . . ." (7). Or, more dramatically, "Flesh experiences time as a singular event—something outside the routine of coming and going: an event which is not a link in a chain but a break, an interruption, an accident, a swerve, fall . . ." (9) No wonder the war reporter wants to be there on the front lines. No wonder the art historian keeps returning to his seat in the museum. To look and feel and wait to see, to be seen.

Some walls cannot be scaled by optimism.

The sensorium transforms into a crisis zone.

"Kill it" writes Alice Notley, "for the human area is over."

Here where we have always been.

Destroyed Works (or, Expanded Cinema)

The textured walls of the old museum are as expected as the hole in the heel of your sock on the Sunday before Passover with pussy willow stalks in a vase in the paint-peeled bathrooms of off-center performance spaces under street lamps set low during recessions.

The rubber plant's water-needs are by now as obvious as my unexpressed longing to return to the foundation of a house in a field by the sea to eat apples fallen from an ancient tree while my mother cuts chunks of cheese with a pocket knife before illness.

A sustained belief in private revelations drives the editor to press his hand against the low back of the author while hedging his doubts about the irrational excess of anyone familiar with the demented Diggers and Ranters of the seventeenth century as she bends forward to adjust her strap near traffic on Sunday.

Having in this very lifetime fallen into spiritual companionship with secular women in succulent costumes especially scarves tied loosely around the empty space of their throats I order nothing but water while gazing into the eyes of enthusiastic young men whose belt buckles glint under their descriptive phrases and impossible histories o the many euphoric eyes.

My fervid glances are as much a brief vital available counterpoint to anxiety as your mouthy effort to persuade us all that there really is a future held within this one a fiery future of sex and cats (not sex with cats) and sloppy sauces that is driving this conversation or should I say conversion so obvious now to anyone who looks for more than a passing second at the trees on our block budding into spring in the morning.

You step now into the shower as if the body is a portion of the soul stationed always at the vanguard of loud bold and deliberately overheated arguments in favor of more weapons in the antechambers within state houses all across our gleaming nation our gloaming nation our giddy nation of harm.

I'm at the wrong desk for reinserting love back into the philosophy of knowledge though every person is free to desire and purchase ointments affections and magazines while undressing themselves in offices or at the edges of quarries where granite plummets into seagull-rich water and little children leap and squeal and every person is free to surge up into the "movement of love" long before any intellectual probing begins, to discover such love with the 2/3 majority who favor absolute freedom for arms.

Uninhibited also are our pregnant girls sauntering front-loaded down our hallways while crystals and roses adorn their dressers at home.

Little girl with a penis she doesn't like stands at the chain-link with her fingers hooked her bare arms shine in a Colorado spring while my girl says she has a small penis her boy cousin a slightly bigger one refusing to bathe and the one thing I disagree with is the urge toward aphorism.

I turn to page 14 of the enthusiasm manual with doubtful fingers.

Despite inevitable structural tensions I'm going to the gym since emotion is pre-cognitive "inherently alien" and all there in the thought of a girl walking outside just as a car door slams or in the moment of breathing deeply right when you read the word "breathe."

Even as I woke from a dream in which lice were crawling all over my head and one by one I flicked them onto a white cloth then scratched my head for a while until switching on the light I had a craving for the mouth of the museum curator with his piercing blue eyes his trousers hovering above sockless ankles his charge the "fashion wing" a wing that could not bore me more entirely love set you going like a fat gold watch I thought in his direction—but are such moods transpersonal? Private? Can they at once be both?

Only 30 minutes left to find a way to melt the animosities springing up within my social group but there are books I can read and faces I cannot and yours is one of those I cannot under the bare light bulb or in the rising dawn make my way in any way toward.

My paths flower-strewn and palms waving while waves palm their own foam and trued wheel spins into alley wind o gentlemen—I am speaking as if across a great chasm as linoleum tells back the shine from gemstones or plastic sequins glued to little girls' sweatshirts and stuck within their hair o gentleman I must admit it is my intention to rewrite your constitution whole.

Guns are good Christmas presents for Mormons I read as the various princesses in my house whether carrying foxes or butterflies riding bison or bikes whether favoring Italian or French pastries especially proclaim their disapproval but who's listening.

The deleted city must be archived and re-imaged in the parking lot of the school for un-gifted children where grasses speed their own departure in a March wind when no rain falls again and again.

I confess here and now to liking the shape of my own lips as they enact the future of feeling on a minor scale my focus as narrow as my ambition is grand but these are ideas we have encountered before so perhaps it's time to alter my font?

Moods might be transpersonal but then writing might occlude one mood while pretending to offer another just as the sea presents a wave over and atop the one that only seconds before was prominently displayed as its best forward effort and each breath overtakes the last until panting and flushed I forgive myself these compromises for there is no other way.

The Light of Is Is: On Anger

The "recalibration theory of anger" posits that anger is developed through the process of natural selection as an effective bargaining tool

Or, anger is simply an alternate way out of difficulty "when all other ways are blocked"

Or, "we were trying to master our fear to calm our anger to restrain our weeping"

When thinking about anger, I see my mother. Is this true of you?

I'm stuck in a font, my "compass." Can't get around that bouquet, delicate tendrils and shoots

Was told many times as a child, "It's OK to be angry!"

Lilies lose their verve; that crack in the cup lets nothing out. Glass and tin, sequins and drill bits, mixed drinks and sexologies directed by teens: this is my garden of earthly delay. My gigs my lap my luster

We are trying to raise a son raise a daughter raise a garden raise a son a daughter a daughter a garden trying to raise a son a daughter a garden

Studies show stronger men and more attractive women are more anger-prone, feel more entitled to better treatment, and prevail more in conflicts of interest

The president is derided for not being "angry enough"

"When we turn from anger, we turn from insight" says Audre Lorde

Or maybe, "the creation of an 'enemy' is a loss"

Such a thought undermines theories that attribute anger and aggression primarily to frustration, a history of negative treatment, or a desire for equity

Strength and beauty are not unique: anything that increases the social bargaining power of an individual should increase her or his anger-proneness and feeling of entitlement

Then there's the "State-trait anger scale"

Entirely contingent, the body of a little girl, hanging around the house with not much breathing space

In the margin to my left is a butcher and a noose forever muffled like winter trees: labiacal

My mother was neither tall nor beautiful

In the jargon of the eighties she was a "rage addict"

My adolescent son grips his head at the table and then, quite literally, screams

Still others say that anger in its "legitimate form" has its roots in feelings of injustice

If hereby I drill into the earth a hole big enough to deposit myself and my children, what dictionary could define us then? What camera record us?

In the jargon of the seventies she was a "strong woman" (not necessarily a positive thing)

"Aristotle's term for the in-irascible person is 'slave' or 'fool,' persons who do not become angry when we expect them to are, in our day, more likely to be described as 'repressed'"

One might have said, and I did say (to myself) that my mother's anger had everything to do with the holocaust and so was genetic

"In the social foreclosure of grief we might find what fuels . . .violence"

(As to my left, a butcher, muffled)

I began to keep a "headache notebook" in which I wrote down everything I ate or drank and the time of eating or drinking, then whether I had a headache or not, and the level from 1-10 of that pain

One might have said, and I did say (to myself) that my mother's anger had everything to do with her feminism and so was justified

One might have said, and I did say (to myself) that my mother's anger had everything to do with her father's anger and so was inherited

At the same time I began to keep a "race diary" in which I wrote down every social encounter I had during every day, the name or occupation of the person I was encountering, the level of intimacy between us on a scale of 1-10, and the race of that person

One might have said, and I did say (to myself) that my mother's anger had everything to do with my father's supposed infidelity and so was retributive

One might have said, and I did say (to myself) that my mother's anger was only the flip side of her great capacity for joy and so was necessary

One might have said, and I did say (to myself) that my mother's anger was not "about me" and so was bearable

To my left, winter trees

One might have said, and I did say (to myself) that my mother's anger was a motive cause of her activism and so was heroic

One might have said, and I did say (to myself) that my mother's anger was an expression of her fear and so was forgivable

Sometimes on approaching our front door, my heart would begin to race

My husband asked me whether the "headache journal" and the "race diary" were connected, since I'd started them on the same day and whenever I wrote in one, I also wrote in the other

A common belief is that children who experience high levels of rage in the home repeat these patterns in their own homes as adults

The rain falling now for seven days with one pause for sun

The rain falling now for seven days with one pause

Anger is an "object" mood, whereas depression is not

I had to admit that the two journals were connected, but I wasn't sure how

I thought I might discover in what way they were connected once I had completed the one-month cycle I had committed to

The failure of the Jews to "resist" or "rebel" is often attributed to a failure of anger or simply to too much trust: "We were German!"

But the Jews I grew up with subsequently were anything but trusting

"Animated"

Chatter of something eating in the heating vent. The cold outside is unfathomable and stuck. Windows become violent, and foreign. I feel afraid

The first and most noticeable thing about my "race diary" is that I very rarely rate my intimacy level to be higher than a four

The second most noticeable thing about my "race diary" is that I often do not know how to classify a person's race

But what would I do about your anger? said one boyfriend upon breaking up with me

In an attempt to be "not angry" I hit my head against the bathroom wall

"I only knew three means to employ, which are always useless and frequently ruinous to children: argument, sentiment, anger" confessed Rousseau

The first most noticeable thing about my headache diary is that my head hurts every single day

Often when I am angry I wonder how my face looks and figure it does not look good.
Do men ever figure that?

Rousseau: "All women possess the art of concealing their anger, especially when it is strong"

The third most noticeable thing about my "race diary" is that I do not know what constitutes a social encounter

"I finally stopped being angry when I realized," begins the memoir, begins the memoir, begins the memoir

The second most noticeable thing about my "headache diary" is that I do not know how to rate pain

She "finally stopped being angry" only a few years before she got sick

A terribly brief "reprise"

Ruinous children undo themselves in the harsh light of what is

She had "calmed her anger" only to find fear the master, and weeping unrestrained

Trying to raise a son, raise a daughter, a daughter, a garden. And in the margins branches heave

Envy

If you are living inside an object, but animated, an animated object placing its alternately cold and hot foot on your cheek, you might feel yourself approaching a melancholic cordoning off, a sense of isolation and claustrophobia at once, much like a man in a cubicle with Johnny Cash pinned to his wall, but female.

Immediately upon being asked to write about the self, most women will turn their attention to another. To their mother, perhaps, or lover. Tree bark, whether rough or smooth, loose or tight, like skin to the self has the pretense of only containing, of not really being, the tree.

Walking up to the bedroom, I count the marks on the wall, slowing my step so as not to miss a single one. Similarly, walking to meet the envied one for dinner, I create a complex graph of types, keeping track of all those with walkers or wheelchairs, all those with beards, all those with glasses, all those with children, so that the effort to keep these evolving numbers clear in my head obliterates the image of his face.

Envy, though perhaps not useless, desires to be expressed or released, to "get off my neck." "Not everything is a competition," says the mother to her daughter who claims passionately to have been cheated out of sugar. A particular situation of "not having" might lead a person to examine the object she thinks she desires with more scrupulous attention than she brings to her own skin, safe in the mirror.

If turning to the envy that colors jaws alternately hot and cold, or, if approaching a melancholic cordoning off of time as if in a cubicle—burn your journal.

"Her daughter was a yellow dowdy, full of envy and ill nature, and, in short, was much the same mould as her mother," we read. Whether in Denver or Brooklyn, none would dispute that the bark of the tree, like the eye or throat, seems to contain something other than itself, something truer, maybe better.

"And why would envy automatically be assumed to be unwarranted?"

Walking to the bedroom, I count the marks. Walking to dinner, I keep track of all those with stick, crutch, or chair, all those with hair. To keep all these numbers clear in my head almost releases me. "Not everything," says the mother to the furious girl, "is for you." Cheated, once again, out of an equal or greater dose of sugar.

A particular situation of "not having" might bring a person to examine more closely the object she thinks she desires with even more scrupulous attention that she brings to her own kin.

Yet "no degree of acquiring what the envied other has . . . will ever culminate in the other and one becoming indistinguishable."

That the rain in films and the emotional suffering expressed in the shot of a closing eye are different orders of suffering than that of crying in the bathroom goes without saying, for the closing of the lid has no scent. The filmed woman unbuttoning her coat also has no scent, no "stench of the present." Once, having been "tossed aside," I resorted to payphones, to multiple calls from a seaside town throughout one whole wet spring day, leaving messages of increasing panic; but just as rain can't fill the ocean because the ocean is already full, no particular event of "not having" can increase envy's store. One way to sooth envy is to draw pictures of horses. Another is to answer a kid calling you from bed.

Some women receive the news of their own near erasure from philosophy and young-adult novels alike as an inevitable layering on of blankets. To withdraw from access like a succulent in a drought feels the most opulent of choices, the most rich. But this "striking out" by no means exhausts what they are.

This work of rubbing envy like you rub the grease on your fingers—with money or clothes, in stores and bedrooms, classrooms and forests, in distraction or hurry—this is a theology. For flexed desire is the thing we'll call divine.

Destroyed Works 2

Theories of labor and theories of experience encourage me to notice my body very utilitarian except when dancing when I might marvel at the presence of four limbs and a torso or when with hands in the dirt the scent of metal floats off the skin, might marvel more and more but not say.

With this motor attached to it the noun moves around, and so do feelings, as if welling and subsiding were the natural effects of time on things and emotions, which they are, for movement makes excess felt, writes Erin, as if in stillness, though there is no stillness, we would have but not feel our excesses, whether they be rage, grief or joy, or pain, brightness, cold, but as there is no stillness there is no way to test this hypothesis except to say that maybe movement, by which I mean gross bodily movement, not the involuntary breath, digestion, and firing of nerves, is always a way to make tangible and more experiential the excesses that are happening at all times in the inner body and mind, and now such distinctions between inner and outer, between involuntary and voluntary, seem arbitrary, even false, a function not of being, but of language, in which one word positions itself against another, like poles in a tee-pee or colors in a painting, leaning on or depending on one another for the formation, always temporary and fragile, of some whole.

One way to see an object, even a moving one, like a woman on crutches arriving for coffee with her mother and siblings, is detail by detail, first a blur of grey and then the thud and creak of the crutch—because one would have to include listening as part of seeing just as smell is a component, perhaps the larger component, of taste—and then the coppery streaks in her hair and the tilt of her smile toward the various others in her group, all of this before even knowing or saying to oneself, a woman on crutches, a disorienting way to perceive, a slowing down of the process of understanding we hold so dear, more dear in fact than the gathering of family members with their matched laughter, or mothers who have been successful at not estranging any of their adult children yet, as if the beauty and seeming happiness of her children were matters of her own volition, as if she were responsible for the snow and for the light gleaming off the wood, the wood carrying the light to her eyes, a kind of fire forming itself in the brain, even as nostalgia rising from a song on the radio overwhelms all these perceptions, for memory is the only way we know we really were the children we were, and not some other child crawling under a table or dancing on the bed to some other musical score, memory is, in fact, the one method we have for proving the existence of time, so that, really, she was my mother once.

Pity Pride and Shame: A Memoir

If food had a desire for furniture and steered the car in a new direction, I was game or passive, I was tasting death on the back of my tongue as if coffee, I was thinking of the one who accompanies me on all journeys. Never too tired or busy to come, she loves to see the world.

I am game and I am passive, but that I feel as I write this a kind
the passive of obligation to the keyboard, the same as I feel toward the kids. I cannot allow them to fail to do something I have told them to do. Cannot allow the keyboard its freedoms. On the History Channel sits a poet I know who has written about Warhol,
sky about pity and pride, for even the night-sky shines with filmed faces. (And I to a man, a man not seen.) On the wall above, a shot of my son and his cousin playing in a hotel in Ann Arbor, and also, a poem by my dear friend. The children grin like monkeys, and just over their heads, a sign: "No Horseplay," which makes me wonder the vintage. The children in horseplay are pleased, aware that they defy. Spit of fire, hooves of

flame. The poet on TV: a pinkish shirt, top button open, hair

fixed up: made to stand for Gay America? I made if different?

In me read.

in me read

This poet is also a pianist, though not like that pianist in Cali-

fornia who held a brand of loneliness you might want to veer

from. As a mall or a wave. A doll or a knave. Let sound the I;

done had use for! I only swallow lumps of earth, as dumb as

proud.

pride of

earth

He played the piano in the other room. I was not charmed, was

distracted, was distracted. As tribute to his enormous skill, I

put him in my verse novel. In this novel he is married, has two

sons, and is still lonely, lonely because the woman he married

is not actually a woman. She is an idea—the idea of Love. (In

memory myself and the all around men.) I modeled her after

a woman I know whose aura is beatific—maternal—in the

broadest sense. A woman on whose lap one wants to rest one's

head. If you do, however, the strangest thing ever—she will not

have a lap. Her maternal aura will evaporate if you attempt to

aura

tribute

fog vortex

approach. For this reason she attracts people like no one I've ever met.

Cloud mass at the summit: a food then a fog. Her husband has mastered this art of not approaching. So too have many of her friends. Let unworthiness; each frankness be the better. I began to sense that she was not what she seemed. Or she was exactly that, exactly what she seemed. Was a "seeming" self. All aura. Like a saint. This was good: she was a vortex around which other people circled. We would call this community, but I don't know how common we were, how caring.

When you die, begins the poem, there are bales of hay. Most British poems from the 19th century are about death. The Lucy Poems, Christabel, The Ancient Mariner, Ode to a Nightingale, In Memoriam. Rolled round in earth's diurnal course. Speaking of these poems, I began to get bored of saying the word "death." Mouth-full of fodder, of food. I precedent, I likeness of I. Years later, she and I went to the Blake show—was aware of her hip; perhaps there was pain there? In a room with French airs on the Upper East Side, private school teenagers in their *excess* extravagant clothing: the road of excess leads to the palace of wisdom. Then, not long after, or maybe before, I went to the same Blake exhibition alone. Stood before a print of Urizen, a man ran a finger along the back of my neck. Someone from the gym. The sudden intimacy disturbing: Of Innocence. Of Experience.

Read "The Tyger" to my children: heat in the rhythms of it. I any to any, I different. I not. When I read this poem to first-

dread graders in The Bronx, they had no problem with the vocabu-
lary. Needed the word "symmetry" explained ("symmetri" to
rhyme with "eye")—but aspire, seize, sinews, anvil, dread,
none seemed an issue. What human is there who does not un-
derstand "The forests of the night"? There is none. This used to
be my son's favorite poem. Now "A Hymn to the Sun" in which
the night is described as a black velvet gown being torn apart!
Is this a sign of adolescence? My daughter prefers O'Hara's
"Talking to the Sun"— the sun, a saucy pedantic wretch. In me,
mold of present. Flare of pride, of hers or the sun's, flaming out
like foil shook. Have I anything in the lack of truth? Been I to
sublime other?

A NEW IDOLATRY

Yesterday dogs in prisons in Connecticut and Indiana: to discipline prisoners, to bite them until they agree to be disciplined, for instance, to get out of their cells. Didn't surprise me: should have surprised me. As earth is wormed is warmed with wrath. Connecticut's an awful state. And I without a my in that. Forgive me, there I've found only shame—dancing on a temporary stage at a street fair. Or sucking my thumb in public as a child—suddenly the thumb in my mouth and no way to pretend it wasn't. Or a party of drunken pre-teens. Spit-slick and reddened. My friend is not jaded; this I admire. But she's afraid of losing her hold on optimism, the optimism that mothering demands. Know any venture can be made a day. She says she must stay on top, must not let things go, but by holding on she is risking faith.

red

public

suck

This is what happened to Wordsworth when England went to war with France. He was more than disappointed—"Thus strangely did I war against myself; / A bigot to a new idolatry / Did like a monk who hath foresworn the world / Zealously

faith

labour to cut off my heart / From all the sources of her former strength; / And as, by simple waving of a wand, / The wizard instantaneously dissolves / Palace or grove, even so did I unsoul." He's talking about not writing, about losing faith in his imagination as he loses faith in the logic of the world. As *forswear* the world becomes an ongoing violence, an illogic, he responds, not by going further into the illogic and wizardry of poetry, but by withdrawing, like a monk. But to withdraw is to enter neither imagination nor reason and what is that? That is to be unsouled; the school of unsoul.

I judge I. I, what good? I interpolated, made, had, an I?

Faces in rows, ears tuned to ditties of no tone. Prof. Cary Plotkin stood before us, singing "adieu adieu" and "happy happy!" I zealously labored to laugh, to see if he would also laugh. And *fled is that* he did which is why now I continue to think of him, to worry *happy happy* that he, like Keats, might have suffered death's advances in Italy, where he, like Keats, went to attempt to heal.

Sorrow keeps breaking in—says Winnie

Saying, now, I obliterate myself, like Keats, become "not my-self," last night would have been the precise right time to do so. My task so clearly before me required the least of myself *speech* possible: to respond to and maintain dialogue with the person I loved first in the world but whose conversing abilities now are hauntingly impeded. This is not meant formally, meant honestly. But even more unselving than struggling to keep up conversation with my mother, with whom conversation was once most like conversing with myself, is the curious unselv-ing of finding myself a temporary stranger to my sister. (I a *stranger* likeness to the truth the I made.) At two, she stood at my back, wrapped legs around mine, placed feet on my feet so I walked her around. This the first intimacy between us, the core of how I know her.

Lying on the couch in the other sister's apartment, I called the friend of the hay poem. "When you die / there are bales of hay." She has had another stroke, she tells me, and is very tired.

She's all right, but is very tired. But very. And are not I dif-
ferent? A poem, as yet unwritten, threatening to stay so, most
fragile, most necessary: chip of an eggshell, lying in the grass.

fall

Pity is treason, said Robespierre, and if pity is the virtue of

spit

prostitutes—Nietzsche—then it is also the virtue of the child

pity

shamming pity. A dying bird chirps in the bush. Suzy taught
me to draw spit lines down my face—to make it look as if I'd

bird

been crying—so that when the police arrived they would pity
us and perform a pity-dance for the bird, which we would

pity

know to be false, but which, we hoped, they would believe us
in need of, and sincerely grateful for. They, we hoped, would
not know that we pitied them for pitying us, for we needed

fog

no pity, we were already masters of irony. But for that reason
precisely, we needed their pity all the more. The child, like the
prostitute, must play a role in order to be fed and maintains
integrity through the pretense of sincerity. And I'd only been
the it before.

If I only I in memory, am coming down the side of a mountain.

I hear one friend say to the other, "But I love being Christian."

This is awesome to me in a very real sense. I, like Wordsworth

at the peak of Snowdon, with nothing to call myself. The fog

spread out below me, obscuring the descent, my mind an

abyss attempting to reform itself. Truth immaterial. That false

I, high-minded. I   exaggerate. But if I do not disbelieve or   *flag*

sublimate   otherwise translate her comment into one I can stand before, I

find myself estranged.

The conversation flags. I am afraid, most of all, of our mother's

estrangement, her loneliness, of ours. I am appalled, most of all,

by the manner with which we discuss work, finance, travel—

all topics now out of her reach. Like a brown paper bag of pota-

toes stored in the cupboard, sprouting near-translucent tubers:

"Fair seed-time had my soul, and I grew up / Fostered alike by

beauty and by fear"

it says.

MORE OF THE SAME

slow

If on an airplane with a few hours to unveil the soul? And I do not speak? I undertaking which imitator? *The Economist* unfolded, and his job to make real estate deals for a bank. Then, the soul might be found in childhood, or a few years back, in a college history class? All those laps. All that weight, lifted.

job

Before the I: my men, near descent? And why not glimpse the

thigh

soul of one's death-partners? But I do a slow job of it; too much skiing, too many restaurants, too much thigh muscle to travel through. Or I haven't started soon enough and soon we will be landing. I have only begun the stripping, the stripping of matter, the unleaving. "For Christ plays in ten thousand places / Lovely in limbs, and lovely in eyes not his / To the Father through the features of men's faces." Have belief make an I at least!

eyes

My stepfather removes his glasses, rubs his eyes; he rubs them for a long time. This concerns me. I eat a potato, and my mother eats a potato. The rubbing of the eyes, a kind of weeping. (Nature wrong in the will.) Or less: a way to remove oneself from the outer scene. For though a very common gesture, common to those who wear glasses especially, it is, when carried on for a while, a kind of escape. As if the person has left the room, has refused, in leaving, to enter any other room. Before this I, I do not mean to overstate.

"More of the same." This was the answer he gave, while rowing a boat, to the question "What do you wish for?" To me, a young teen, this was preposterous. I stared. Not one other person in the boat, and perhaps there were six of us, all of us, would have said that, would ever say that, could say that now. It was as if he knew he would not have it. But while more of the same seemed the most humble, self-effacing and undemanding of requests, it was, of course, the most extravagant wish imaginable, the most impossible. Like wishing for fairies or for God. Mine, though tossed at stars and into fountains, though blown at fire, were not fantastic. Love and Fame though they will sink to nothingness, dropped from the hand of chance. (Embellishments only fill lacks.)

A television actor named Katherine instructs me to get a phi-

losophy. Her mother, like mine, sinks into the "twilight" of

twilight   dementia. The philosophy of clothes comes to mind. (Be myself

and myself sublime!) In which we realize that clothes are not

really clothes. We've touched on this before. The desire to strip

and knowing there can be no stripping since we are already

stripped. But then why must *The Economist* be set down before

the soul of the child announces itself a lover of history? I am

my prejudices. He was hungry, and this unveiled him as my

son. If only there was less mass in the thigh. My son eating a
                                                                        meat
drumstick says "yum." He must share it with his sister, and he

does, as he has shared everything since the day she was born,

but music and reading. These have been his privacy. (Round of

hear *my my*.) The privacy of the book, so much like the privacy

of rubbing one's eyes. She returns the bone, stripped of meat.

Thanks, he says, and lays it next to his plate—continues to

empty the pods of their tiny peas. They pile up, food for a baby,

who prefers pear, scooped from the soft center. (With secrets.)

One does not worry oneself over the soul of a baby. The baby

laughs at rhythm. I learned this when at five I made my sis-
ter laugh by pretending, repeatedly, to sneeze. It was not the   *happy happy*
sneeze but the repetition. They hear it, they expect it, and
when it comes again, it's funny. (The *and*!) Pleasure in repeti-
tion. This is laughter at "more of the same." As if even the
infant knows this is a pure dream. (A child portion.)

(I am without. Never desire.)

But then the snow comes. And at the same time, a sewer-like
stench up from the pipes. We sleep, but always with this dual
awareness: the thick wet whiteness "blanketing," the offen-

flame & sive odor "wafting." And why? (And find desire.) My husband
suggests some kind of squeezing action (and find desire): the
snow exerts a pressure on the earth—and poof, out comes this

dirt gas. "Like the ooze of oil / Crushed." In the early mornings my
fingers sometimes have trouble pressing the right keys. I must
forgive myself my errors. (My nature.) You might think this
easy, but it is not. With the figure of a woman buried in dirt to
her neck uttering disconnected words in sets of three always
now before me—self-forgiveness becomes a hard task. Sidney *a blight*
said his heart was slamming in his chest as he read Beckett's
Happy Days. On the drive to work only shyly do we mention
the true and intense enthusiasm we feel for these artifacts. Ex-
uberance more embarrassing, in the end, than failures to iden-
tify, failures to have read. As if exuberance a blight. (Myself I,
I am, not seen.)

Mountains rise up and hit you in the face. This too is taken as eventless. Believe not. Instead we discuss Fred the Fed in Paris. His partner—and I'm not sure in what sense—is an x-quarterback from Texas who gave up football to study child psychology, then gave that up to move to Paris for drugs. A *gun* long and tortured path. When high he'd grow passionate about child psychology. Fred the Fed was mostly silent. And it was he, and not the massive Texan, who was dangerous. He'd carry a gun. (Whether rightly destroying?) Sidney, trained in passive resistance, had no familiarity with guns. Fred would leave the gun sitting there on the kitchen table. They called him Fred the Fed because of his demeanor, because of his immobile features. My son, on the other hand, has a face like water. (Which can ever after be read.)

On TV the politicians rub their eyes. Captured at their desks *wow* with foreheads leaning on the edges of their hands, or captured rubbing their eyes. Entering the no-space of unsouling. This because the war is not going well. (Of judgment: will *myself* judge.) Online one can play at war. You know this, but perhaps you do not know that there are blogs where you can, as a Lieutenant, a Private, or even a General, write the script of the war that is alongside the real war. (In will, will is done.) That is to say, dead Afghanis, dead American soldiers, wounded ones needing treatment, strategies, homesickness, dissent, confusion: Wow! That was fast! Hell! That was faster than a Pokémon Centre! you say. And your partner answers, You're right! Wow! In this game-war you use game-metaphors to describe your game-experience. The layers of artifice are baffling! Wow! When mid-sized, my son and his friend would have played Pokémon for fifteen hours without stopping if we'd let them. The friend claimed to do precisely this at home: Pokémon on his Game Boy while watching Pokémon movies, while eating dinner, while tying his shoes, while doing his homework. (Good with bad.) We found this disturbing, but he did not have a mother. This is not accurate, nor is it fair.

war against

myself

In my verse novel, I struggled with whether L, the seeming woman, should have children. Her real-life model has children, but it was difficult for me to make sense of her absence and

diamond

her maternity at once. For while she was the figure of pure

maternal aura, she was not, in fact, capable of mothering. This

is because she had a vanishing lap, as I've said. Lady Eustace

has a child and it annoys me that Trollope seems to forget about

him for dozens of pages at a time. (Gap memory.) Currently,

Lady Eustace is in Scotland at her castle. She has brought the

diamonds of course but it is unclear whether she has brought

the child—the child who is only two. The problem with the di-

amonds is that they are legally *his*, but she wants to keep them.

This little invisible boy is the center of the novel, is the novel's

main character. Because he is a boy, he does not need to be

seen in order to dominate. Poor Lady Eustace must be seen and

seen and seen again. (Assume a false I.) I understand Trollope's

point, but one wishes to be informed as to the whereabouts of

the child. And so, in my verse novel, I include children, and

then worry about them. Brood. Like the Holy Ghost. Brooding

over the bent world. (Myself false, high-minded.)

His mother was living in a neighboring city, but she had lost

custody. There are few things a woman can do to lose custo-

boy

ghost

dy of her child. We do not want to know. We would rather hear about Fred the Fed and his gun. (And/or have a self.) One would rather read the game-war. When he badly scraped his knee, though his father was there, I bent down, I applied the Band-Aid. Later, I was ashamed. Did I mean to imply that the father was not capable of applying? (Lament.) Did I mean to appear, in this way, attractive to the father? Something was off. Did I mean to critique the absent mother? I knew myself to be false even as I bandaged him. (And imperfections revealed.) The snow and the stench.

absent lament

After snow she is sick. We send her to school anyway and she
is sicker. Now we have to pay and she has to pay. (I commenc-
ing.) We are greedy about time. (Hitherto and.) When I am

sick

proud I laugh at myself. When ashamed I also laugh at myself.
But this laughter is more pride, and more shame. (Imitator of
my likeness.) The shame/pride effect. It has to do with being
ignored and feeling ashamed of oneself for being so present in
other people's way. "Not untwist slack they may be these last
strands of man / In me." The dawn is rosy. Despite the snow
the trees still wear their orange dresses. But once ignored, once
in this way alone, you finally know that you are a self, and for
this reason, you are proud. Her sickness is a kind of gift, for
she lies in my lap quietly and listens to stories. Does not yell

slack

out or demand things. My I I made.

And not destroying. Giving over to the body of another? Lying,
as she does, in my lap, not struggling, listening? Not untwist.

FOR THE DAY IS BREAKING

In darkness I move myself around. Dreamed I had married the

photographer who proposed on Church St. (I commencing.) I

laughed, I am ashamed to say, and he threw the flowers down.

I remember sex with him better than I remember sex with any-

grief   one else but my husband, and why is that? In the dream I am

no longer concerned about appearances. This was one of the

hard and fast   problems. (And will be.) But my grief is that I have not since

met a person whose sense of humor hits quite the same vein.

His favorite foods: mustard, olives, and oh no, I have forgotten!

(Find imitator.) My sadness is that I have forgotten the third

food: garlic or wine or salt? (Desire set.) The pigeons silver   *pepper*

in the sun—flapping up off the black roof of the neighboring

building. (All true nature that.) And why is that? When it was

hard and fast and sad.

Saw him on the subway and my heart leapt up. Searched that

and found immediately someone's blog-post called "My Favor-

ite Ex." Only a favorite ex makes the heart leap up? Is a favorite   *game boy* ex somehow like a rainbow? A covenant between the self and the self's ability to love, to have loved? She, Sheila the blogger, writes, "soak up my memories," and "beautiful tree-lined street." This makes me stop.

dust Currently. I wake in the dark and move myself around. Little assessment. Brood. The bird's wings. The mind of love is brooding. Death comes and replaces desire. Rightly, wrongly, destroying my mold. The pigeons circling.

My loneliest friend knows many Biblical verses. I am ashamed to say I do not. "Jacob was left alone; and a man wrestled with him until daybreak. When the man saw that he did not prevail against Jacob, he struck him on the hip socket; and Jacob's hip was put out of joint as he wrestled with him. Then he said, 'Let me go, for the day is breaking.' But Jacob said, 'I will not let you go, unless you bless me.' So he said to him, 'What is your name?' And he said, 'Jacob.' Then the man said, 'You shall no longer be called Jacob, but Israel, for you have striven with God and with humans, and have prevailed' . . . Therefore to

striven &
believing

no

this day the Israelites do not eat the thigh muscle that is on the hip socket, because he struck Jacob on the hip socket at the thigh muscle." The thigh muscle, you will remember, stood between myself and the soul of my row partner. If I had known I would have thought differently.

broken But maybe it's time to let all this go. The naming and the wrestling. (Judgment.) The naming and renaming of the self. Maybe it's time instead for the giving over of the self. (When will will myself?) I give myself to you, for you I must lie down and be quiet.

But if calling out repeatedly from bed and the one you are

calling does not answer? (I.) The snow has melted and yes-

terday we drove upward to find it. (Am commencing.) A boy

we brought with us was miserable. He cried; he threw snow   *wind*

at us, then, when we threw some back, he lay in the snow

and cried. I should have been more patient. (An undertaking

hitherto without.) Now all the pink is gone from the sky. This

happened suddenly between cries, and if only I were kinder.

(Which will never). When snow enters your collar or cuffs it is

torturous. When does one learn to withstand this pain with no

comment? (Find an imitator.) This comes with the awareness

of mortality—because death is the loss of the heat-producing

mechanism, we value the signs of that presence? (I desire to set

before my fellows.) We are warm and then we will be cold. For

now, warm: "till death or distance buys them quite. / Death or

distance soon consumes them: wind."

The haunted house was called "Deadville." My children were

too afraid to enter. (In all the truth.) This surprised me. One

wants to "be dead" for Halloween. (And that.) Something ter-

rible happened when I applied the dead-flesh makeup to his

skin: he looked dead and I wanted to sob. (Man.) He also, I

think, wanted to sob, which is why, maybe, he would not enter.

(Myself, myself.) Here comes the other with a jar of vitamins

and a red-lipped smile. Three goodbyes later she is gone. (My-

self alone!)

flesh

After crying in the snow, the boy pogoed around his house

high on sugar and no food. (I know the feelings of.) The father

stirs the meal, the father turns the TV off; in the sudden calm

of no screen, there is nowhere to stand or sit, and only plati-

tudes to speak. And only platitudes to speak. (My heart and I).

The dog howls. A homesickness.

"I need a belt / A big one. // I am old / very old // I come from

California / And I am going back," our boy wrote at 9.

flesh / belt Even as we make childhoods like meals we eat them. (Know men). I am not made like any. Disrupt that: That light sasses the trees and a far away chimney. We who have chimneys, we who have trees. Didn't I write that when I was a girl and how did it find its way here? Paper is decrepit: decay is in your hands.

(I have seen.)

wings

By beauty and by fear: on narrative time

I. FEAR

"A window," writes Cole Swensen, "is a mode of travel . . . flying sleeves" (10). But here, gray rectangles of gray dawn—nothing more, nothing moves. Still in the bed, having slept hardly at all. A homemade dollhouse mocks me with its cardboard beds and paper rugs. A plaster wedding cake on the floor, a jumble of heels and skirts.

Back in the library sits a cart of photography books, each more gruesome than the last. I told the librarians I was researching violence, and am embarrassed by how seriously they took me. In fact, I am researching my own fears. Every childhood is marked by qualities, and though I'm not proud of this, the quality I recall most often is that of fear. I had nothing too obvious, nothing too bodily, to fear. Nonetheless, most of my earliest memories, and many of those that follow—

The vines at the window, the threads that unraveled from my blanket, the cats I lived with, the fireplace, and the dark wood of the floor. The cupboards and the backs of drawers, my brother's hands and my mother's mouth.

*

Insomnia plagues the fearful.

"What is it to be a *who* or a *me*, or even more radically, a *no one*: without identity, that is, no longer able to say 'I'?" asks Gerald Bruns in *On Ceasing to be Human* where he examines various claims of non-self-identity that run through twentieth-century philosophy. Sleep, he argues, seems to offer the escape from the self that is both longed for and feared (*On Ceasing*, 3). Sleep—the house of the unnarratable I.

Bruns has also written on Wordsworth's fear, here in the line from *The Prelude* I've borrowed to title this essay. And for Bruns, the fear Wordsworth explores throughout *Lyrical Ballads* and also in *The Prelude* is less the fear of not being an *I* than that of becoming another: "the fear that intimacy with another mind carries with it [is] a risk of transformation into the strange, the monstrous, the more-or-less-than . . . human" (*Hermeneutics* 171). To encounter the monstrous in a book, in the streets, or in your mother is to experience the terror that one might become, one might in fact already be, this one who murders, this one who raves.[2]

I could not sleep because of fear, because the year I spent reading websites and staring at photography books that featured some of the most monstrous things humans do to others was also

---

[2]And it should be admitted Wordsworth's others are marked primarily by poverty, monstrous to him for the affliction of not having as often as they are afflicted with madness or sorrow.

the year my mother shat in the furnace room when she could not find the bathroom, the year she wandered the house sobbing "miserable, miserable" to herself or to us. The year I lost her to miserable was the same year I spent in the archives of American violence, as if one set of fears might outshine another. Of course I feared losing her to misery. Of course I also feared losing myself, to her misery or to my own, or to the misery that is all of ours—a particular American misery. Perhaps not sleeping became a way to protect, with avid intensity, the fiction of the coherent narratable self, this temporary invention of the day.

Calm succumbs to the hour . . .An embedded immensity fills you . . .
There is no self just this falling off. (Claudia Rankine, "Airplane")

John Lucas's camera has filmed the soft faces of people asleep on planes, sky drifting past. Claudia calls sleep "the inevitable move inward" but inward toward what, if in sleeping I "lose myself"? "Isn't this confidence? / Isn't this the completed life?" she asks as they float.

*

At fifteen in an airport alone I picked up a payphone to call my friend Kate. She answered from a room in which she and her parents and brother had just learned that her other brother, the other twin, had been killed. A room: from Latin "rus," or "open land." I hung up the phone and redirected myself into that room where un-poured Coke and Sprite sat gleaming in candlelight. Kate's mother with her hand at her mouth. Everyone looking at nothing but the floor. That floor, that open open.

And now, decades later, another friend from that time—she's the one staring at nothing. An SUV jumped the curb where she was walking with her two sons. The older one, ten, a slight boy with dimples in his grin, was struck and taken. In another airport, some dim hallway, I stand trying to breathe, my forehead against a carpeted wall. TSA workers kindly pass me by.

Ever since I started to track it, I watch from the distance of intact motherhood the parade of parents whose faces we fear for fearing we will wear them.

Some deaths are accidents, some are not, some accidents are lies.

*

It's been said that poetry can reverse the movement of time—for when you get to the end of the line, you have to go back to the beginning again. "Our eyes darting from the end of one line to the beginning of another create a kind of instability in linear time," says Chris Nealon paraphrasing J.H. Prynne (no pag.). It's also been said that poetry ruptures time—makes a hole in the movement of time we call "day" or "hour." This happens when language is so thick and complex that to read is to get caught in traps and ruts. All those "little knots of impacted, concentrated, dense language: paradoxes, ambiguities, and indeterminacies; self-reference and repetition" writes Cathy Gallagher, "seem to cross back and forth over [themselves] and consequently to thwart forward movement" (Gallagher 247). Complexity and recurrence—more than literary devices—a refusal of directed velocity.

A poem, perhaps, is an anti-narrative, which might be a good reason to fear it:

> and so an instant can really get intense
>
> through forceful concentration
>
> forcefully knotted
>
> And its emotion is only rooted
>
> in the certainty of accident   (Nicolas Pesques, *Juliology* 6)

*

A swell of laughter from across the room: the conspiratorial laughter of colleagues. My mother, counting all her losses, the foremost among them, linear time, said that what she most longed for was a "colleague." It was hard for her to remember this word—but it was an important word, I realize now, because a colleague is that person who shares in your process of narrating the self. A colleague assists you in making a fiction, a fictional self. A family member's intimacy reveals the failures of that fiction. A family member knows too much about accident and error, and anyway, intrudes, makes a mess of you. Maybe this is why telling your life story to people on buses and planes, your passing, temporary colleagues, is such a drug.

2. NAME

"How's the baby?" I ask. "Doing good, doing good. But he's doing that day/night reversal thing." Because the wind is blowing, we keep the conversation short. The baby's wrapped up but for his little face, his shut tight eyes. Clouds amassing in the west, turning the blue sky dark. Babies are good, but they stay up all night. The wind is blowing. They haven't yet given him a name.

Why must the Queen in the fairytale, trying to save her baby, guess the little man's name? A name out of nowhere, an untraceable, unlocatable, unrootable nonsense name could never *be* guessed. It would be like trying to see a color that does not exist. Though the story says, "He took pity on her," on her maternal terror, it's obvious that by asking her to guess his impossible name he is showing her exactly no pity. But the Queen is no innocent either, for Kingly greed has infected her; once "humble, meek, and grateful," now, despite her promises, she's greedy for her child. And her greed directs her to cheat, to use her power, her servants, to find out the little man's name. She wins in the end, which means the baby wins his permanent home and eventual kingdom (for don't forget, this baby is the heir). But this winning is a result of deception, which is perhaps a fact of all kingdoms—won through lies, by way of lying, just as pity is a lie. A pretty pitiless tale.

The little man never thought for a moment that she'd guess his name (and he was right about that). He exposed himself, however, by the fire. Confessions—burned out of us as dance and song.

And yet, the name is not just a riddle that once solved will land the Queen safely in the country of mothers; it's also a curse, for once spoken it destroys the little man. He flies off through the window on a spoon and is "never heard from again," or, in the darker versions, he's so enraged he stamps a hole in the earth and is sucked down into it. Unbirthed: taken back into the body. The little man—the baby's doppelganger—is the unnamed, the unnamed one who must be destroyed in order to complete the narrative, in order to reinforce (patriarchal) order, which relies on names.

So what happens when my friends finally name the baby boy? Is something lost at that moment, even when so much is gained? Does the baby, in taking on a name, become, in some other way, swallowed? Blake:

> "I have no name;
>
> I am but two days old."
>
> What shall I call thee?

> "I happy am,
>
> Joy is my name."
>
> Sweet joy befall thee!

That verb "befall" hints at the crisis that circles the act of naming. The verb dates back to Old English (897), and seems to have meant simply "to fall" until the 12th century where it begins to also mean "to inherit"—which is certainly one of Blake's meanings here. But as I search the OED I find that almost all instances of "befall," where it takes an indirect object ("thee"), indicate an inheritance that is bad or dangerous—that will leave its object worse off, not better.

"I do not know what it gives," wrote H.D. of the "jewel" vibrating at the center of her poem "Tribute to the Angels": "a vibration that we can not name, // for there is no name for it; / my patron said, 'name it'; // I said, I can not name it, there is no name" (*Trilogy* 76). Patrons, kings, queens—need things named. Poets, though they trade in words (or because they do), recognize and defend the unnameable core that burns.

Before named, the infant of Blake's poem is pure happiness. Language can't even organize itself correctly around that happiness (I happy am). But once named, once "called," it suffers a fall, one could say, into narrative. No easy opposition, then, between the fear of no narrative and the comfort of having one. Because as soon as you begin to tell yourself, something of yourself is lost. And not all narratives, dear mothers and fathers, dear children, end well.

*

Cloud mounds. Heaps. Masses. And the little lifted screens click and hum. One could turn things off, but not the sky. One could read the entire newspaper start to finish. Start to finish. Mouth to foot. So I said to my head, go on. One could visit the green edges of the mind in cafés where one talks to oneself through the keys. There, on a rickety chair, a woman sat picking at her food and told me a story.

The last thing she said was, "He finished the job," as if we were in a movie.

The story is about a man who was sleeping on her mother-in-law's couch. Her mother-in-law was helping him out because he was having some troubles. They were both in Houston for a time, "finishing a job" in order to earn their pensions. The mother-in-law hadn't told anyone about the guy on her couch, and, it seems, hadn't been aware that he was using. He was just a co-worker, a friend, and he too had left his family behind to follow this job—his wife and five kids. Something about this story feels incomplete. Everything about this confession is borrowed. He killed her, says the woman across from me, with a kitchen knife. He stabbed her over nine times. "Finished the job."

The son, my friend's husband, makes plans to visit a firing range in order to learn how to shoot. This is perhaps a reasonable response. Perhaps not.

That night, I can't sleep. My head hurts and I'm awake at three. In the glow of the lamplight, I read two stories.

The first is narrated by a ghost. The ghost watches while a wealthy eccentric old man has sex with his (the ghost's) dead body. Because the ghost is beyond caring about his body, he empathizes with the old man's suffering and befriends him, listens to him through the night as the old man confesses to, and attempts to explain, his depravity.

In the second story, a boy witnesses the slow death of his older brother. The brother, dying of cancer, is nonetheless cruel and violent. And when he can no longer behave violently, he does so by proxy—has a friend hurl a padlock at his younger brother's face. What do these stories have in common? What do they share with the story told in the café? Depraved, sick, lonely and lost boys and men. The standard situation for narratives.

"Let me in," say the women, picking at their food.

*

They named him Owen.

Once he is named he begins to have a face. Once he has a face, he will begin to make sounds other than instinctual. He will begin with vowels, and they will rise, as Plath said, like balloons.

*

Not sleeping might be an illness, or it might be a symptom. A product or a producer of fear. The unnamed little man at the fire will take your child. Only the vigilance of insomnia will allow you to hunt down his name, will keep your kid safe, and keep you too in the story. But after a number of weeks of not really sleeping, I begin to fear, not just the nights, but the days too.

3. BEAUTY

Fair seed-time had my soul, and I grew up

Fostered alike by beauty and by fear (*The Prelude* I: 301–2)

The beautiful and the fearful (or the sublime, as the mother of fear) are the two dominant aesthetic

categories during Wordsworth's time. One might say his effort throughout *The Prelude* is to work

out their relation. Fear, he suggests, turns its ear outward, listening for external threat:

I heard among the solitary hills

Low breathings coming after me, and sounds

Of undistinguishable motion, steps

Almost as silent as the turf they trod.

...

With what strange utterance did the loud dry wind

Blow through my ear! (I: 322-25; 337-38)

But beauty, it seems, when not referring to some transitory attribute of a girl, lad or sky, wells up

from within, is the mind's answer to sublime terror, the mind's imaginative ability to reorganize,

or "harmonize"—to make coherent sense out of what it fears:

Dust as we are, the immortal spirit grows

Like harmony in music; there is a dark

Inscrutable workmanship that reconciles

Discordant elements, makes them cling together

In one society. (I:340-44)

Elsewhere Wordsworth calls beauty an "ennobling Harmony" (VII: 771). But more famous and more bold is Wordsworth's triumph at the very end of Book XIV where, having confronted the "fixed, abysmal, gloomy, breathing-place"—the earth, which he earlier refers to as "an enemy" (30) —he now declares the mind of man "A thousand times more beautiful than the earth / On which he dwells" (449–50). The mind, "in beauty exalted" (454) imbued with imagination, spells the end of fear: "For there fear ends" (163).

But what if pulling beauty apart from sublime terror is not an option?

What if beauty cannot tame fear, for the feared thing and the beautiful thing are one?

An older allegory serves me better: Hephaestus, the ugly forger of technologies, was in a rage against his beautiful wife's promiscuity. The net he wove of gossamer thin wire was meant to capture Aphrodite in the act of betraying him. But when he trapped her and her lover, the irascible and violent Ares, the other Gods gathered around and only laughed and laughed.

That gossamer net forged with precision is one way to understand narrative. And beauty, which rises out of foam, defies the traps narrative sets for it. She has, as the story tells us, more affinity with violence than with the "inscrutable workmanship" of craft. According to Homer, the entrapment only leads Aphrodite to divorce Hephaestus, for in the *Iliad* she "consorts freely with Ares." And so beauty slips out of the grip of craft and into the arms of brutality.

*

It's been said that our name is our first story; I learned to paint mine on an easel, steadying myself with letters. At that time the song I loved to sing most was "Michael Row Your Boat." I loved it, then, because of milk and honey, and for the comfort of its names: Michael, Brother, Sister. I love it now for other reasons.

As in many of the African American spirituals, the words might give instruction from slave to slave on how to access freedom, how to break out of the story that has been written for you: don't talk about it, don't boast, code it in song. The song or the poem creates a momentary erasable bridge when the structural bridge is not there and is too dangerous or impossible to build. "In the end what I'm interested in is precisely that transference, a carrying or crossing over, that takes place on the bridge of lost matter, lost maternity, lost body and its ephemeral if productive force," writes

Fred Moten reading Frederick Douglass reading slave song (Moten, *In the Break* 18).

Michael's boat's a music boat: the fragile, temporary, wild-built beauty of song set loose in a four-year-old mind that knows nothing yet of the stolen lives that made that song and sings it not to taste that bitterness but to taste something sweet, something luxurious, tasting the bitter nonetheless.

> Wild Nights—Wild Nights!
>
> Were I with thee
>
> Wild Nights should be
>
> Our luxury! (Dickinson 120)

I read that too once I could read. And it's Dickinson who said of beauty "Chase and it ceases"; like wind in the grasses, you can't overtake it. Fear she called a stimulus, an impetus, and a spur. One draws you forward, the other pushes you from behind, but it's that same wind on either side. Put your boat into that wild storm: "Done with the Compass — / Done with the Chart!" — that Eden.

*

Once I started sleeping again and found myself an ordinary person, riding buses and drinking coffee, standing around in a singular body in that endless Denver sun, I was stunned by my own presence, its bright dailyness. Sidewalks felt hard again under my feet, the air sharper, my senses were re-revealed. That sounds emotional. It was, but it was also physical. One morning the sky was all Easter, so pink and salmon, so baby blue, I thought it must be kidding. Going for a walk, making a meal, it all seemed obscene. Obscene because what had scared me, my mother's misery, the country's misery behind and before the gun, these twin terrors, had gone nowhere, they only got worse. But I was back to belonging because I had to be, or because I could be, and it did and didn't seem all right.

There really is no poem outside of fear, no sublime on one page and beauty on the other. To write is to call to that fear, to lie down in it. Or to put it more bluntly, the terror of the un-narratable, un-nameable "I" that I encounter in my mother's mind full of holes, is fucking the beauty I want—the anarchic violent poem.

*

So I end with and in my mother again, who raged out of fear and feared her rages, and who now, with no narratives left ("discarding the ceremony of consciousness / drifting into nothing") is, one could say, no longer a mother—who, without linear time, can no longer scare me and no longer love

131

me. And if she's no longer a mother, than I'm no longer a child—now a dead child. But maybe emotions, once set into action, continue indefinitely like entropic molecules, even after the person who "felt" the emotion can no longer "feel" it or say it or know it. Maybe love stands outside of narrative, antagonistic to story—like language, just something people walk into, row out into. Is love, then, a condition, rather than a feeling? Like language, a condition, not of the person, but of the world?

That's not me: an afterthought

August 2013

Dear F and all:

Yesterday afternoon it poured for ten minutes flat. Then on and off all evening long. Capricious sky. Three friends performed Wallace Shawn's *The Designated Mourner* in our living room. "Frank" murdered himself. This thing called the self, he strangled it, choked it, destroyed it. After that, he was free to experience pleasure. Pleasure came in the form of pornography first, and then later, the bloods and oozes of fall and an evening breeze. The audience was mostly under twenty. What did they think of murdering the self (but keeping the body around)? One of them is interning at the Governor's office. He's working on Homelessness Initiatives but he didn't know about Denver's camping ban. Or, he'd heard of it, but he thought it was just a way to move people off the 16th street mall (like pieces in a game of checkers, just slide them off the board). The camping ban criminalizes sleeping outside. If, that is, you are covered. If you want to just go ahead and fall asleep, like a baby in a stroller or a person at a picnic, you can do that. But if you cover yourself up with a blanket or any other kind of covering (cardboard, tarp), well, you can't do that.

Linda didn't watch the play. She sat out on the porch in the rain as it softened to mist. Just the day before I'd said to another friend, "Linda knows what she wants and what she needs better than I do. Sometimes it's a bit disconcerting." My other friend said, "Well, then you don't have to waste time trying to guess." That's true, but I'd wished she'd watched the play so we could have talked about it after, for she's the one I always want to boil tea with. (As her friends at Holy Cross taught her, and as she taught me, "boiling tea" is slang for after-party gossip). One of the actors, the one who played Frank, has written a book about his brother who has schizophrenia, diagnosed when he, the actor, was just a boy. This manuscript is heartbreaking. But he doesn't try to publish it. Now he's writing about poetry's revolutionary dreams. He comes from a family in rural Colorado with very few books. He's been married and divorced and his new girlfriend has a kid, so, like everyone in graduate school, he needs a job. Linda, sitting alone in the rain on the porch, also has a brother who suffers. And she also grew up in a home with very few books. And she's also been divorced. Maybe if she'd known about my friend's real life she would have come inside to listen to Frank, whose been assigned to grieve.

The other actor has a condition with his ears. All the time he's hearing things. Sounds like a vacuum cleaner going on directly into his ears, or like the whine of a car engine unable to start. He's hearing horrible sounds directly into his ears all day and all night and no one else can hear them. Over these sounds he can sometimes hear you speak, sometimes not. As he's speaking in the play, I'm wondering if he's trying to out-sound the horrible sounds that are coming from nowhere, coming from the atmosphere inside his head, that are torturing him day and night so that he can't sleep and can't work, sometimes can't even read or write. He's a teacher by day. He's had to take a lot of time off. What will he do? So in the play he plays Howard, a pedantic, cruel old man. Maybe he is this pedantic, cruel old man for a time, for how can a person escape his own ears?

This week we spoke about sound and intimacy, which made me think about whispering, or the sound of someone kissing you, or breathing into your ear at night. It also made me think of languages we invent as children hiding in closets or as poets in our partnerships, our gatherings. We wanted a new word for intimacy, just like we wanted a new word for "self," and we got "impetus." "Impetus" is a Latin word and it means, or meant, assault, violent impulse, onslaught. Maybe this is not really what we wanted. In the middle of the 17th century, the age of John Donne, it comes to mean directional force. Sound too can be a violence. As can intimacy, as you said.

John Donne played an important part in *The Designated Mourner*. Though the actors never read or quoted from a John Donne poem, they spoke about him a lot as a stand-in for "culture," this thing that would be lost once all the "Power" was destroyed. The story going on behind the scenes is one of revolution in which the poor (the "dirt eaters" as the play calls them) rise up and murder the rich—systematically shoot them or slash their throats. And what is lost when this happens is a population of people who appreciate Rembrandt and read John Donne. This is all very Matthew Arnold—meaning this is exactly what Matthew Arnold feared—that the poor would, in gaining power, destroy "culture." But you played us Richard Burton reading Donne's "St Lucie's Day" not in order to preserve their cultures exactly, but in order, maybe like Shawn, to allow us to consider that poetry is always interested in the murder of the self.

Which is one way a poem might help us to reimagine what is common.

In that poem Donne names the earth "hydroptic," a word transforming during his time, a malleable term. As an earlier form of "dropsical" (so it seems) it means waterlogged, though what he's getting at in the poem is "insatiably thirsty"—dropsical's other meaning—as he describes the Earth on winter solstice. Beginning with metaphors of light, Donne moves quickly to metaphors of thirst: the setting sun empties its flask (shakes it out in the form of rays), and now the world, having drunk, thirsts for light in darkness.

But the poem is not about the Earth, or not only. Donne describes this dying sun and this dry earth in order to say that he is more nothing than they are. He is "every dead thing," first ruined, then "re-begot" "of absence, darkness, death: things which are not." Having lost his lover, Donne negates himself, makes of himself a grave for death, a hole for a hole.

Confessions like this one in Donne, those confessions of self-negation, self-effusion, and self-evacuation that so abound in poetry, might serve a cathartic urge, but they could serve a political purpose too, as you suggested, cutting us loose, even momentarily, from our steadfast attachment to being selves that the law names, granted the equivocal privilege of ownership, the uneven privilege of "rights."

But I want to come at this poem another way, to look at the immediate cause of Donne's self-disavowal. For it is love, this force that's clearly stronger than sun or earth, which has "ruin'd" him, unmade him in order to remake him as a hole, as its hole. He retains then a kind of self, maybe a kind self—a self as a space for longing, a place for the other to reside, even in her absence. A self possessed, not self-possessed. It's what I've wanted to be.

It's what I was trying to say about the mother/child: that there is not, in that relation, any singularity in a simple sense. I don't want to speak for the child side, but for the one who holds, carries, bears, and releases without ever really losing, though never fully having, the other. So rather than turning to the familiar claim that my self is multiple, I'd say in some moments I've know myself as a passage through which others move. Maybe this is a way of thinking through the problem of the self that my sex makes available to me, but I know you were right there too when you talked about why you don't want your sons running out into the street: because to lose one would be to lose yourself. As Butler puts it: "It's not as if an 'I' exists independently over here and then simply loses a 'you' over there, especially if the attachment to 'you' composes part of what 'I' am."

That motherhood is a release of self would be one way to say it, except that this is so often not the case. I could just say less heroically that it sometimes reminds me that I was never whole to begin with, but am passage and a passing. But then I believe motherhood to belong to you too, and to everyone who could say, like Donne says, love killed me and then it remade me out of the nothing I had become.

I wondered if the kids in the room that day, kids who are still someone's child, no one's parent, knew what the hell we were talking about. Maybe it takes a long time to know what risks you carry. But you don't have to lose a child or beloved to know it; you just have to know that you can lose one. Which you know the minute you have one.

"I, by Love's limbec, am the grave / Of all, that's nothing," writes Donne. "Limbec" is the still used in the alchemical process. Love's limbec, then, is the method or tool love uses to transform the liquid in the lover's body into something else, or nothing else, to, in fact, vaporize the liquid in the lover's body so that he can become that emptied-out hole. What makes poets in particular want to have or be or perform this "nothing" so badly? "I am nobody, who are you?" I read when I was eight and kept it by the bed. "I nothing am" says Edgar, hiding in the body of another. Sometimes I've thought it's the freedom that comes with language, language's vapor-like qualities, how it's nothing and can be everything, that we start to identify with, want to not just use but *be*—like Keats climbing up to his muse Moneta and begging to peer into her hollow brain, to see through her eyes that see nothing, or like Plath on Ariel becoming foam. But right now I think it's more than that. It's a spiritual longing, but it's a political longing too. As you said, or as I think you said, in emptying out the self, in alchemizing it into vapor, we get to that complicated word: empathy. But you've said a lot more than you did that day about nothingness and blackness: "If the slave is, in the end and in essence, nothing, what remains is the necessity of an investigation of that nothingness. What is the nothingness, which is to say the blackness, of the slave that is not reducible to what they did, though what they did is irreducible in it?" Forgive me for circling this nothingness in your work not knowing if ever there is a way in and knowing too that I am already in it, not only because of the complexity, the unwinding, of your sentences, from which I find myself unable to turn, but also because blackness is the term in your work I can't and don't want to move off of. How can I get in, asked the very young white woman in our class (she was not even twenty), and you said, come with me. I thought that was generous then, a kind of empathy, a kindness, and now I think it was also inevitable: as in, unavoidable. Already in it.

2.

And so I should start today talking about Trayvon Martin, his name in a hard spot in a whole lot of minds, even more now that we've heard him screaming. Did you read Charles Blow's devastating essay? "Now what will I say to my sons?" he writes. I was sitting in the airport as my daughters were boarding a plane to fly to New York without me, and when I read this plaintive line, I looked up.

A man nearby was watching his two sons board that same plane. I could tell by his face that it was the end of the "Daddy visit" and he was devastated. But he was white like me, so that I was thinking in his direction, "but we don't have to ask today, 'Now what will I say to my sons?'" He was devastated watching that plane take off, but he wouldn't even look at me for commiseration— though I would have been miserable with him if he'd tried. Maybe he was ashamed, ashamed of devastation, as am I.

"What appears in shame is precisely the fact of being riveted to oneself," writes Levinas. Though that riveting is perhaps not a fact but a fear. Just at these moments of division when who you are is so clearly distinct from who someone else is, when your son walks free and her son is shot, there's a necessary shame in that, in being riveted, just sitting there in a plastic chair with it, your body, what it is or isn't.

To say like Donne says that you're a space for another, the hole that can hold someone, not just in arms, but in the belly, or the ass—this shame-infused space of desire that can't really ever be met is what I'd call the fantasy of motherhood. Which I continue to choose.

Once a long time ago I'd had my heart broken. I was walking along a little bridge with one of my teachers, a woman named Nancy with a braid down her back that reached all the way to her butt crack. Walking along behind her with marshy grass on either side of the bridge, I watched the braid gracing her ass like the bridge winding through the grasses. Without turning around she said, having your heart broken is just like falling in love. In both instances something breaks and you're in the world more fully. It almost doesn't matter, she said, whether you've just fallen in love or just had your heart broken. Either way, split, you're alive.

My face was broke before they came, held by what I didn't hold

before they got here and tried to take me. "Is this you?" they said.

"Naw," I said, "that's not me."

That's you in the poem "Modern Language Day," where you also say, "The clear-eyed want to take my shit."

That being broken, that broken heart or face, it hurts and it makes you "not you," or not recognizable, not available to be taken—a vapor. And being that broken thing, which you are when you know what you have to lose, or what you have already lost, makes you love what's bad—that tent city in your poem, the "irregular" of everybody. Then the shame of being riveted must also be the failure to recognize how you are already broken. Turn that shame around and it's its own kind of broken. Or, said another way, shame marks the hole.

What you said in an interview I read, quoting Baraka, is that "art is a sliding away from the proposed," and you connect that to Adorno's phrase: "art's immigrant law of motion." Maybe what you're getting at is that poetry or art or music lights up that space of not belonging, of not belonging to a self we could ever call one. Art's sliding immigrant status shows us where the holes are, or shows us the holes we are.

Recently a friend of mine curated an art-exhibit about homelessness and home and he called it Not Exactly. I kept thinking this was not such a great title. It doesn't exactly say much, Not Exactly, not exactly letting people know what the show is about. The show featured art by people who have homes and people who don't, by people who have shelter but no home (like prison inmates), and people who have home but no shelter, like some un-housed people who don't want to go to the shelters, who don't "exactly" feel homeless. Not Exactly, now I realize, is a really good name for the show, refusing, as it does, the force and the freeze of definition. It's like

"'Is this you?' they said. / 'Naw,' I said, 'that's not me.'"

Love,

Julie

NOTES

"Pity, Pride and Shame" is an experiment in autobiography laced with fragments of Romanticism. It was created in concert with *The Confessions* of Jean-Jacques Rousseau. Each of the nine sections borrows language from the first page of Book I of Rousseau's work. Rousseau's words (Orson translation) are selected through a mathematical process that I have since forgotten, and are inserted in increasing frequency through the sections.

"That's not me: an afterthought" began as a letter to Fred Moten, written in August of 2013. Fred had just taught a workshop at The University of Naropa's Summer Writing Program, which I attended. The letter was a direct response, or outpouring, to our class. Also attending: Linda Norton, Derrick Mund, Richard Froude, Mathias Svalina, and others.

ACKNOWLEDGMENTS

Objects from a Borrowed Confession: The phrase comes from my long-time collaborator and friend, dance artist K.J. Holmes, who invented it as the title for a dance theater piece that will use my unpublished verse novel *The Seduction of L* as a text. I borrow it here with her generous permission and in enduring gratitude for her friendship and love and for our work together. Not me without you.

Thank you also to deeply valued readers, writers and collaborators: Alexis Almeida, Aaron Angello, Michele Battiste, Gerald Bruns, Sidney Goldfarb, Steven Goldsmith, Laird Hunt, Chad Kautzer, Ruth Ellen Kocher, Kevin Kopelson, Sara Marshall, Rusty Morrison, Fred Moten, Linda Norton, Jennifer Pap, John-Michael Rivera, Tim Roberts, Margaret Ronda, Selah Saterstrom, Eleni Sikelianos, Sasha Steensen, Mathias Svalina, Roberto Tejada, Ronaldo Wilson, and Andrew Zawacki. And thank you especially to Janet Holmes for her dedication and support.

Great thanks to Andy Fitch at Essay Press, Josh Wilkinson and Afton Wilky at *The Volta*, Mónica de la Torre at *BOMB*, Rebecca Wolff at *Fence*, and Christian Peet at *Tarpaulin Sky* for publishing portions of this book in earlier versions.

QUOTATIONS

"The sky and earth in their lust seem small on this naked body of water." Trai, 14

"try to show you what is inside myself—a freak, a foible, a mental illness if you like." Hugo Von Hofmannsthal, 118

"I've written about this quite often over the years, but I always forget it. I am my brain. Whenever I remember this . . . the thought simultaneously fills me with horror and wonder, while also raising all sorts of ethical questions as to how I should live my life." Levi Bryant, Larval Subjects Blog, March 8, 2012

"summers without flowers, daughters without mothers, and sea without produce." Morrigan's prophecy

"There was once a miller who had a beautiful daughter." "The Robber Bridegroom," retold from *Grimm's Fairy Tales*

"And I remember well / That in life's everyday appearances / I seemed about this time to gain clear sight / Of a new world." Wordsworth, *The Prelude* XIII 367-370: 1850

"We should aim at the Infinite but tangentially, rebounding on the curvature of light in order to change planets." Jacques Darras, correspondence

"One of the questions I bring to this: are there more skies, more heavens, than the one we see?" This line and the essay that follows are derived, but not directly quoted from Jean-Luc Nancy's lectures to children, collected in *God, Justice, Love, Beauty: Four Little Dialogues*

"The laborious opera concerning how we came to name the eternal." Saterstrom, no pag.

"Aristotle's term for the in-irascible person is 'slave' or 'fool,' persons who do not become angry when we expect them to are, in our day, more likely to be described as 'repressed.'" Ngai, 183

"In the social foreclosure of grief we might find what fuels...violence." Butler, *The Psychic Life of Power*, 183

"And why would envy automatically be assumed to be unwarranted?" Ngai, 128, slightly altered

"No degree of acquiring what the envied other has . . . will ever culminate in the other and one becoming indistinguishable." Ngai, 173

"When you die / there are bales of hay." Valentine, 250

"Thus strangely did I war against myself; / A bigot to a new idolatry / Did like a monk who hath forsworn the world / Zealously labour to cut off my heart / From all the sources of her former strength; / And as, by simple waving of a wand, / The wizard instantaneously dissolves / Palace or grove, even so did I unsoul." Wordsworth, *The Prelude* XI: 74–81: 1805

"Fair seed time had my soul, and I grew up / Fostered alike by beauty and by fear." Wordsworth, *The Prelude* I: 305-06: 1805

"For Christ plays in ten thousand places / Lovely in limbs, and lovely in eyes not his / To the Father through the features of men's faces." Hopkins, "As Kingfishers Catch Fire"

"Like the ooze of oil / Crushed." Hopkins, "God's Grandeur"

"Not untwist—slack they may be—these last strands of man / In me." Hopkins, "Carrion Comfort"

"till death or distance buys them quite. / Death or distance soon consumes them: wind." Hopkins, "The Lantern Out of Doors"

"It's not as if an 'I' exists independently over here and then simply loses a 'you' over there, especially if the attachment to 'you' composes part of what 'I' am." Butler, *Precarious* 22

"If the slave is, in the end and in essence, nothing, what remains is the necessity of an investigation of that nothingness. What is the nothingness, which is to say the blackness, of the slave that is not reducible to what they did, though what they did is irreducible in it?" Moten, "Blackness and Nothingness" 744

"Art is a sliding away from the proposed"; "art's immigrant law of motion" Rowell, 963

SOURCES

Augustine, Saint. *Confessions*. Trans. Albert C. Outler http://faculty.georgetown.edu/jod/augustine/conf.pd

Baraka, Amiri, The Roots. "Something in the Way of Things." https://www.youtube.com/watch?v=cW5gOkoz1io

Barthes, Roland. *Mourning Diary*. Hill and Wang, 2012.

Butler, Judith. *Precarious Life: The Powers of Mourning and Violence*. NY: Verso, 2006.

_____. *The Psychic Life of Power: Theories in Subjection*. Stanford: Stanford University Press, 1997.

Bruns, Gerard: "The Senses of St. Augustine (On Some of Lyotard's Remains)" *Religion & Literature*, Vol. 33: 3 (Autumn, 2001): 1–23

_____. *On Ceasing to be Human*. Palo Alto: Stanford University Press, 2010

_____. "Wordsworth at the Limit of Romantic Hermeneutics" *Hermeneutics Ancient and Modern*. New Haven: Yale University Press, 1992: 159–178.

Caputo, John and Michael J. Scanlon, Eds. *Augustine and Postmodernism: Confessions and Circumfession*. Bloomington: Indiana University Press, 2005.

Clark, T.J. *The Sight of Death: An Experiment in Art Writing*. New Haven: Yale University Press, 2008.

Derrida, Jacques. *Jacques Derrida (Religion and Postmodernism)*. Trans. Geoffrey Bennington. Chicago: University of Chicago Press, 1999.

Dickinson, Emily. *The Poems of Emily Dickinson: Reading Edition*. R.W. Franklin, Ed. Cambridge: Belknap Press, 2005.

Flaubert, Gustave. *Madame Bovary*. Trans. Eleanor Marx-Aveling. http://www.gutenberg.org/files/2413/2413-h/2413-h.htm

Gallagher, Catherine. "Formalism in Time" *MLQ* 61.1 (March 2000): 230–251.

Gellhorn, Martha. *Selected Letters of Martha Gellhorn*. Ed. Caroline Moorehead. NY: Holt, 2007.

H.D. *Trilogy*. New York: New Directions, 1998.

Hopkins, Gerard Manley: http://www.bartleby.com/126/49.html

Keats, John. "The Fall of Hyperion": http://www.bartleby.com/126/49.html

Levinas, Emmanuel. *On Escape*. Trans. Bettina Bergo. Palo Alto: Stanford University Press, 2003.

Lyotard, Jean-Francois. *The Confessions of Augustine*. Palo Alto: Stanford University Press, 2000.

_____. "The Sublime and the Avant-Garde" *The Differend: Phrases in Dispute*. Trans. Georges Van Den Abbeele. Minneapolis: U of Minnesota P, 1988.

Miller, D.A. "Vertigo." *Film Quarterly*. Vol. 62:2 (Winter 2008): 12–18.

Moten, Fred. *Hughson's Tavern*. Providence: Leon Works, 2008.

_____. *In The Break: The Aesthetics of the Black Radical Tradition*. Minneapolis: University of Minnesota Press, 2003.

_____. "Blackness and Nothingness (Mysticism in the Flesh)." *The South Atlantic Quarterly* 112:4, Fall 2013 (737–780)

Nancy, Jean-Luc. *God, Justice, Love, Beauty: Four Little Dialogues*. Trans. Sarah Clift. NY: Fordham University Press, 2011.

Nealon, Christopher. "The Prynne Reflex" Claudius App: http://theclaudiusapp.com/4-nealon.html

Notley, Alice. *In the Pines*. NY: Penguin, 2007.

Ngai, Sianne. *Ugly Feelings*. Cambridge: Harvard University Press, 2007.

Pesques, Nicholas. *Juliology*. Trans. Cole Swensen. Denver: Counterpath Press, 2008.

Rankine, Claudia and John Lucas. "Situation 2" http://claudiarankine.com/

Rousseau, Jean-Jacques. *Confessions*. http://www.gutenberg.org/files/3913/3913-h/3913-h.htm

Rowell, Charles H. "'Words Don't Go There': An Interview with Fred Moten." *Callaloo*, Volume 27, Number 4, Fall 2004: 954–966.

Saterstrom, Selah. *Ideal Suggestions: Essays in Divinatory Poetics*. Laramie: Essay Press, 2016

Sedgwick, Eve Kosofsky. *Touching Feeling: Affect, Pedagogy, Performativity*. Durham: Duke University Press, 2003.

Swensen, Cole. *The Glass Age*. Farmington, ME: Alice James Books, 2007.

Trai, Nguyen. *Beyond the Court Gate: Selected Poems*. Paul Hoover and Nguyen Do, Trans. Denver: Counterpath Press, 2010.

Valentine, Jean. *Door in the Mountain: New and Collected Poems, 1965–2003*. Middletown, CT: Wesleyan University Press, 2004.

Von Hofmannsthal, Hugo. *The Lord Chandos Letter: And Other Writings*. Trans. Joel Rotenberg. NY: NY Review of Books, 2005.

Wordsworth, William. *The Prelude*. http://www.bartleby.com/145/ww286.html

JULIE CARR is the author of six books of poetry, most recently *100 Notes on Violence* (an Ahsahta Press Sawtooth Prize winner), *RAG,* and *Think Tank*. She is also the author of *Surface Tension: Ruptural Time and the Poetics of Desire in Late Victorian Poetry* and the co-translator of Leslie Kaplan's *Excess—The Factory*. She regularly collaborates with dance artist K.J. Holmes and is the co-founder of Counterpath Press and Counterpath Gallery.

AHSAHTA PRESS

NEW SERIES

AHSAHTA PRESS

SAWTOOTH POETRY PRIZE SERIES

2002: Aaron McCollough, *Welkin* (Brenda Hillman, judge)
2003: Graham Foust, *Leave the Room to Itself* (Joe Wenderoth, judge)
2004: Noah Eli Gordon, *The Area of Sound Called the Subtone* (Claudia Rankine, judge)
2005: Karla Kelsey, *Knowledge, Forms, The Aviary* (Carolyn Forché, judge)
2006: Paige Ackerson-Kiely, *In No One's Land* (D. A. Powell, judge)
2007: Rusty Morrison, *the true keeps calm biding its story* (Peter Gizzi, judge)
2008: Barbara Maloutas, *the whole Marie* (C. D. Wright, judge)
2009: Julie Carr, *100 Notes on Violence* (Rae Armantrout, judge)
2010: James Meetze, *Dayglo* (Terrance Hayes, judge)
2011: Karen Rigby, *Chinoiserie* (Paul Hoover, judge)
2012: T. Zachary Cotler, *Sonnets to the Humans* (Heather McHugh, judge)
2013: David Bartone, *Practice on Mountains* (Dan Beachy-Quick, judge)
2014: Aaron Apps, *Dear Herculine* (Mei-mei Berssenbrugge, judge)
2015: Vincent Toro, *Stereo. Island. Mosaic.* (Ed Roberson, judge)
2016: Jennifer Nelson, *Civilization Makes Me Lonely* (Anne Boyer, judge)

This book is set in Apollo MT type with Frutiger Neue titles
by Ahsahta Press at Boise State University.
Cover design by Quemadura.
Book design by Janet Holmes.

AHSAHTA PRESS
2017

JANET HOLMES, DIRECTOR

PATRICIA BOWEN, *intern*
SAM CAMPBELL
KATHRYN JENSEN
COLIN JOHNSON
DAN LAU
MATT NAPLES